THE LANGUAGE
OF SECRECY

THE LANGUAGE OF SECRECY

Symbols & Metaphors
in Poro Ritual

BERYL L. BELLMAN

Rutgers University Press
New Brunswick
New Jersey

Library of Congress Cataloging in Publication Data

Bellman, Beryl Larry, 1941–
The language of secrecy.

Bibliography: p.
Includes index.
1. Kpelle—Rites and ceremonies. 2. Poro (Society).
3. Liberia—Social life and customs.
4. Secrecy. I. Title.
DT630.5.K63B43 1983   302.2   82-13157
ISBN 0-8135-0969-6

Photograph on title page by Lisa Little.
Grebo Mask courtesy of Metropolitan Museum of Art,
The Michael C. Rockefeller Memorial Collection,
Bequest of Nelson A. Rockefeller 1979.

Contents

Foreword

Why do we withhold secrets from one another? And why do we paradoxically relish the conveying of these same secrets to selected others? There is something both obvious and profound in these questions; obvious because secrecy is a ubiquitous part of the human condition, and profound because it implicates something basic in our human nature: that is, as some of the wisest students of that condition have observed, our capacity, for better or for worse, to lie. In the invention of language, we humans obtained an instrument of self-awareness and of negation that enabled us both to deny what is obvious and undeniable to other animals and to prevaricate about our experiences. That power, for the worse, leads to all that is torturous and perversely secretive in the human condition: deceit, deviousness, hypocrisy, chicanery, pretense, dishonesty, unfaithfulness. The lexicons of human languages are full of terms which testify to the disturbing power of prevarication. At the same time, and for the better, that power enables us, as we say in the social sciences, to define situations—to take the "as if" and make of it the "is." Who is to deny that our fictional powers are central to what we humans are and to what we have become. For human creativity lies in our freedom for and our engagement with fiction—the benign form of lying. But even in our power to create fiction, there lies the notion of the secretive—the notion of a profounder reality that our powers of prevarication, whether devious or benign, have concealed or can reveal. The notion of something concealed in experience is profoundly human and arises, it may be argued, from our capacity to lie.

It is obvious that such a profound and paradoxically ambivalent capacity deserves our closest attention. Indeed all human societies have had laboriously to develop ways of managing the power to prevaricate so that the center of things does not fall apart and so that people can hold to each other with some confidence that their mutual expectations will be realized. One of the most important institutions available to human groups for this purpose is ritual, with its particular power to sanctify and thus guarantee human relationships. The paradox is that rituals employ prevarication—benign perhaps—in order to save us from their detrimental consequences. Rituals, of course, are almost always associated with secrets known only to the initiated.

It is the great virtue of Beryl Bellman's cogent and well-argued study of the Poro secret society—and other secret societies—of West Africa to have looked squarely at this paradox, which he calls the "paradox of secrecy." The reader should bear in mind that the materials brought together in this book are not the result of brief field study but the fruit of well over a decade of recurrent fieldwork in Liberia and among Kpelle. In the process, Bellman gained remarkable rapport and exceptional entrance into the secret societies. This has enabled him to follow convincingly through what he calls "the natural history of the secret" in these societies.

What do we learn from such longitudinal study of "a culture where secrecy is the most pervasive concern of daily life?" What do we learn from such a subtle sense of problem as is characteristic of this study? We learn first of all that the content of the secret is not as important as the "doing of secrets," for it is in the activity of the making and conveying of secrets that the various orders and domains of social reality are defined and established. The conveying and withholding of concealed knowledge is not only a way of maintaining privileges in the social order; it is, more fundamentally, a way of establishing its very domains and categories of interaction. A careful study, as well grounded in the local language as is Bellman's, of the "doing of secrets" reveals the processes by which humans negotiate their existence and construct their social realities. In the interaction of the obvious and the hidden—the real and the alternative reality—we gain particular insight into how this reality itself is constituted; for the fact of secrecy and the alternative realities it conceals poses a constant problem of interpretation to the members of a culture. It poses the constant problem of deciding what is relevant. Men and women are constantly having to be aware of, or to find out, the "meaning contexts" in which they are acting and the language, the "what-can be-talked," appropriate to such contexts.

It may be thought that these problems are peculiar to these "secretive societies" in which the institution of the secret society is paramount. In point of fact, the problems of the interpretation of the appropriate contexts of action and communication—the problem of the revealing of the relevant relation between "talk" and context—is a universal problem in human societies. It is simply revealed the more clearly when we study it in secretive societies. There need be no argument here for secrecy per se. But on the other hand, we should not allow our own, quite appropriate, mistrust of secrecy or our view of it as a necessary evil—as in "official secrets acts" or in espionage and counterespionage—to cause us to overlook what we can learn from it, in operation, about the constitution of social reality.

Another instance of Bellman's acute sense of the heart of the problems he poses for himself is his analysis of symbol and metaphor in the "doing of secrecy." There is, no doubt, something essentially secretive and "prevaricating" about both of these figurative devices of human communication, for a symbol, by definition, is a polysemic device, some of whose meanings will always be much less than obvious, if not actually hidden. And a metaphor—a device, after all, that says a something, say a king, is actually a something else, a lion—is an assertion of an alternative and perhaps, heretofore, hidden reality. Bellman shows how the diffuse display of symbols and the more focused assertion of metaphor is central to ritual secrecy and the alternative realities it seeks to define and maintain. He shows us the central place of symbol and metaphor in the creation of the multiple orders of social reality and in the shifting back and forth of these orders. There is much more in this intriguing and well-grounded book than a foreword can or should reveal. Let the reader with any interest in the profoundest problems of human social life proceed with the assurance that many other secrets of that life will be herein revealed.

James W. Fernandez
Princeton University

Preface

In this book I examine a large complex of secret societies associated with a major secret society, Poro, and its female counterpart, Sande, in the West African forest belt culture area, a region of Central West Atlantic Africa (d'Azevedo, 1962) that includes Liberia, southern Sierra Leone, and parts of Guinea and the Ivory Coast. More specifically, I analyze instances in which secrets are communicated within the societies, and I conclude with a focus on the most recent series of initiations into the Poro in one of the important centers of Kpelle secret-society activity, along the Liberia-Guinea border. Because the initiations occur only once every sixteen-to-eighteen years, the initiation period is one during which the concept of secrecy is most problematic for members. This study has a dual purpose. First, by analyzing secrets within a context where secrecy is one of the most prominent organizing principles in daily social life, it is possible to examine the variety of forms that secrets take and thereby isolate secrecy as a phenomenon. In this manner, I call attention to practices that are relevant to the communication of secrets in every culture. Second, I present an investigation of the Poro initiations as a ritual process, and through an analysis of the operations and transformations of the symbols and metaphors used, I provide a detailed account of ritual secrecy in one of the most important secret associations in Africa.

In the first chapter, I develop a theory of secrecy in the context of the literature on the topic. I take the phenomenological, hermeneutical, and ethnomethodological perspectives to demonstrate that secrecy is both observable and analyzable because it is an accomplished interactional phenomenon. I conclude the chapter with a discussion of the methods I used to obtain my data and to analyze the materials presented here. In the following two chapters, I describe the Poro complex of secret societies. I begin with a general discussion of the Poro and consider how it has been able to accommodate different social and political conditions. I then describe the Poro complex of societies as they are practiced among the Fala Kpelle. I focus primarily on two towns, Sucromu and Kpaiyea. These two neighboring communities have significant differences in the way they practice their respective Poro associations. By comparing them, I discuss the ways in which the Poro can structurally vary while at the same time maintain its integrity as a major secret society. This chapter provides the ethnographic detail necessary to an understanding of the symbolism expressed in the course of the rituals discussed in the other chapters of the book.

In the fourth chapter I discuss the concept of secrecy in the secret societies and its significance for the daily life of Kpelle speakers. I describe how secrecy is understood as a process for intentionally structuring the flow and organization of communication. I explain how the warning of Kpelle speakers to "do not talk it" is a constitutive feature in every Kpelle conversation. I discuss how speakers make their decisions about what to say, how to approach a topic, their speaking prerogative, and turn-taking order within different types of social situations.

In the fifth chapter I discuss how secrets can be analyzed as texts. First, I describe a domain of Kpelle speech called *Kpelle wo su βela* ('split Kpelle words'), or "deep Kpelle" or "deep talk." This includes the extensive use in conversation of parables, metaphoric expressions, dilemma tales, and mythical narratives. It is through these different figurative genre that concealed information is adumbratively communicated. I present methods that members use to interpret their intended meanings and to locate the information contained in them.

In the sixth chapter I describe how the methods used to understand "deep talk" also are employed in the interpretation of ritual activities. It is here that I present the sequence of events that constitute the Poro initiations. Two types of rituals are discussed: rituals of illusion and rituals of allusion. The former are those in which participants produce auditory or visual manifestations, creating illusions of such things as the different types of "devils," or *ngamu*; malefic spirits and demons, or *jina*; and ancestral spirits. Rituals of allusion are similar to what Turner (1974) and Fernandez (1977) have each called "ritual metaphors." These are events whose interpretations analogically refer participants to other realms of activity. The different ritual events that constitute the initiations are described according to the range of meanings communicated to different categories of participants.

In the seventh chapter I describe the formal structures of ritual oratory. This involves the analysis of speeches, blessings, parables, and announcements made during different rituals in the initiation process. Translations of segments from three rituals are analyzed to demonstrate the operation of metaphors within them. I discuss how different oratorical methods communicate specific information and concomitantly display the types of structural relationships that exist between the Poro and the community. In the concluding chapter, I discuss how this investigation of secrecy in the Poro contributes to the development of a general theory of secrecy and how it contributes to the sociology of knowledge.

Previously, most discussions of the ritual process of the Poro initiations have been from second-hand accounts and descriptions by untrained observers. I have collected materials on the initiations proper for over four years and have conducted ethnographic research in the same communities for more than thirteen years. Much of the data presented come from audio and video recordings, made by myself and several Kpelle field-research assistants, of many rituals and events concerned with secret-society activity. I was able to witness, and in many cases participate in, the events, and I kept field notes on what occurred. I interviewed all the major participants and had the full cooperation of the Poro leadership throughout this study. Many among the leadership, or Zo, actively participated in the collection of the materials and in the analysis. In this country, I had the benefit of the assistance of two Kpelle research assistants from the communities involved: Mulbah Sumo Jackollie and the late Yakpazuah Bella Tokpah. Finally, after completing my analysis, I returned to the field with relevant portions of my data to verify the work done here.

My research was supported over the past thirteen years by a variety of sources. The research on the Poro initiations was funded by two grants from the Social Science Research Council, a National Endowment for the Humanities Fellowship, and, for the follow-up research, a grant from the Wenner-Gren Foundation. I also received several supplementary grants from the Academic Senate of the University of California at San Diego. Without the generous support of those foundations this study would not have been possible.

In writing this book I had the benefit of discussions with a number of colleagues who also have worked in Liberia or in neighboring countries that have the Poro and Sande. Also, discussions with colleagues in other disciplines have been of great value throughout this work for the advise they offered on the use of theoretical concepts in their respective fields. As the list of such colleagues is extensive, I trust they will forgive me for not mentioning their names. I must, however, thank Marlie Wasserman of Rutgers, who was interested in this book since its inception, for her encouragement and patience. I also thank Marribeth Bernier for her insightful suggestions in the preparation of this manuscript and for her insistance on clear and lucid writing. I am very grateful to Janet Mais for her valuable advise and her painstaking efforts in making final editorial revisions. If unnecessary jargon or an overly pedantic style remains, I bear sole responsibility.

Since writing this book I have had to mourn the death of several of those who are mentioned in it: Mulbah Koplah, the leader, or Zo, of the Snake Society, who was my "stranger father" when I first came to Sucromu; James S. Mulbah, the school principal; Chief Waiquai Vallai, the *loi kalong*, who died shortly after the completion of the initiation rituals; and his son, Flumo, who had just taken over his father's office when he was killed in an automobile accident during a visit to Monrovia. I also grieve the death of my research assistant, Yakpazuah Bella Tokpah, who drowned in a swimming accident while in this country. It is to their memories that I dedicate this book.

THE LANGUAGE
OF SECRECY

1
Introduction

This book is about secrecy. The practice of keeping secrets is pertinent to virtually every kind of social situation in any culture. It serves as an organizing principle for legal and illegal corporate groups (Chrisman, 1974; Lyman, 1964; MacKenzie, 1967; Schaefer, 1980; Shils, 1956; Tefft, 1980b) and provides auspices for informal alliances between persons who share hidden information (Adler and Adler, 1980; Bonacich, 1976; Ponse, 1976; Warren, 1974). Secrecy is always a problematic concern of participants as some are more successful at practicing it than others. Often the complaint is made that someone does not know how to keep a secret. Yet, it is the very nature of secrets that they most often are told. Simmel (1950) describes how a secret is a sociological form that "stands in neutrality above the value functions of its contents" (p. 331). The management of secrecy is invariant to the kinds of information controlled by it. Indeed, those most responsible for the maintenance of security systems need know nothing about the secrets they protect yet are often able to exercise considerable authority over those who do know (Coser, 1963; Lowry, 1972).

Simmel (1950) emphasizes that content is independent of the methods used to conceal information. Most social scientists have, nevertheless, examined secrecy by making typologies based on either content or the consequences that result from the exposure of concealed information. This has resulted in a general confusion over the definition of secrecy and the criteria used to describe it.

The effects of exposing concealed information is the basis of Shils's classic study (1956) that contrasts secrecy with privacy and publicity. He defines *privacy* as "the voluntary withholding of information reinforced by a willing indifference" and *secrecy* as "the compulsory withholding of

3

knowledge, reinforced by the prospect of sanctions for disclosure" (p. 22). He contrasts both with publicity and claims that the three were functionally related and usually in equilibrium. He maintains that when privacy is countered by a strong demand for publicity, there results a marked increase in the desire for secrecy. The obsessive fear of secrets leads to a denial of the right to privacy and to a concomitant rise in the demand for publicity. The acceptance of privacy is accompanied by a lessening of concern with secrecy. Shils uses this model to analyze the rise of McCarthyism and the so-called dread of Communism that has arisen in many postindustrial societies and to explain the different national attitudes about the need for security and official secrecy.

Warren and Laslett (1977) criticize Shils (1956) for not adequately accounting for the sanctions that are also placed on the inappropriate telling of private knowledge. They argue that this confusion would have been avoided had Shils distinguished between "public and private life secrecy" (p. 47). They define the former as secrecy "on the part of those in power and their agents, acting purportedly in the public interest" (p. 47) and private-life secrecy as concerning one's personal life. Thus they argue for a definition of secrecy based on a differentiation of content.

Shils (1956) and Warren and Laslett (1977) each extend Simmel's (1950) observations that secrecy is often associated with evil, and so is "the sociological expression of moral badness" (Simmel, 1950: 331). For Warren and Laslett, secrecy is "the concealment of something which is negatively valued by the excluded audience, and in some instances by the perpetrator as well" (p. 44); and privacy is a way of protecting behaviors that are "either morally neutral or valued by society as well as by the perpetrator" (p. 44). They maintain that "privacy implies the legitimate denial of access, while secrecy in general implies that the denial of access is illegitimate" (p. 45). Shils, likewise, treats secrecy as something that is negatively valued that will decrease in a truly democratic and open society.

The negative values normally attributed to secrecy come from the view that it is a kind of deviant or antisocial behavior. Secrecy is often associated with illegal or extralegal political groups that are either subversive or self-serving at the expense of the larger community and with the subcultures involved with illicit drugs and alternative sexual lifestyles. When secrecy has been studied in bureaucratic settings such as business and government, it is still recognized as having negative implications. It works to stifle cooperation that could lead to greater progress, as did cold-war politics by interfering with scientific research. As Coser (1963) points out, there is a strange paradox involved in the fact that even though secrecy may be considered vital to national security, the shared knowledge of the comparative strengths of all parties is the most effective method of avoiding conflict.

The definition of secrecy as the calculated concealment of information, whether positive, negative, or neutral, encompasses both secrecy and privacy. Tefft (1980b) characterizes secrecy as "a strategy for behavioral adaptation [which involves] the coping mechanisms that humans display in obtaining their wants or adjusting their lives and purposes" (p. 321). He then defines the concept as "the mandatory or voluntary, but calculated concealment of information, activities, or relationships" (p. 321). He distinguishes between what he calls "intimate secrecy," or privacy, private-life secrecy, and public-life secrecy. Each definition is based on a differentiation of content. Hence, for Tefft, privacy is a subcategory of secrecy that deals with the concealment of intimate knowledge. His definition does not account for the distinction that is so apparent when, in answer to a request for information, we are told "That is private" instead of "That is a secret." The former usually establishes that the asker does not have a right to some knowledge because of his or her social distance. A secret, on the other hand, concerns information that the asker may have rights to but that the possessor chooses to, is told to, or is obligated to withhold. The revealing of that information provides grounds for a different interpretation of the social reality. Essentially any item of information can be the content of a secret. What is important is that the knowledge, once obtained, leads to a new definition of the situation. What is private or public depends on factors other than those involved in the practice of secrecy per se.

It is best to consider secrecy, not as a power struggle between those who know and those who want to know, but according to the ways concealed information is revealed. Even the methods used to conceal information involve a revelation to those engaged in protecting it. According to Kermode (1979), who is concerned with secrecy as it is found in literature and biblical parables, the true meaning of a text is always elusive. In his analysis of the Gospel According to Mark he maintains, "We are most unwilling to accept mystery, what cannot be reduced to other and more intelligible forms. Yet that is what we find here; something irreducible, therefore perpetually to be interpreted; not secrets to be found out one by one, but secrecy" (p. 143). In so asserting, he recognizes secrecy's narrative character. Concealment and revelation are similar because the same text is used for both activities. The content is virtually inconsequential to the process.

When information is present as a secret, there is much more to the message than the content. Goffman (1969) speaks of secrets as information about information. He describes the various methods used to acquire, conceal, and reveal information as expression games. A major aspect of expression games is the significance of each participant's knowledge about what is occurring during an interaction where information is controlled.[1] When an observer is denied access to some knowledge to which he might be entitled and when that information provides a different interpretive schema for understanding some reality, the guarded information is called a secret. If the observer learns that information, he often makes the discovery a secret. In both instances, there is the restriction of information about information.

The knowledge that constitutes that restriction is metacommunicative. It is information about elements in the language code rather than the events to which the elements refer.[2] That includes what Hymes (1974) calls the "key" to message forms: how the manner, tone, and spirit of a speech act provide, in part, the schema to interpret its intended meaning. Thus, depending on the key, someone's speech can be taken as a joke, a pun, an analogy, an exaggeration, an irony, a secret, or any one of a number of other intentional forms. Secrecy is metacommunicative because when one hears the telling of a secret there are a number of implicit instructions that accompany it and constitute its key. This includes not only how the talk is to be literally understood but that the information is not to be repeated and that the source of the knowledge is to be protected.

Those tacit instructions establish an interesting paradox. Consider the kind of interaction when a secret is told. Normally the teller prefaces his talk by informing the respondent that the forthcoming information is a secret and must not be repeated. The preface immediately communicates that: (1) the speaker is telling information that is concealed; (2) the occasion of exposing the information is not illegitimate; (3) the teller is trusting the listener not to reveal the information or its source; and (4) the teller can still be trusted as one who can keep a secret even though he or she is engaged in the very activity of telling the hidden information. This creates what, following Goffman (1974), can be referred to as a "double frame." The telling occasion is bracketed as distinct from the normal flow of talk, which itself constitutes a meaning context, or frame. The frame exists within a larger frame. The listener is instructed to disregard the telling as an exposing and to treat the occasion as an exception to the rule of not revealing secrets.

The problem is structurally similar to what has been referred to as the liar's paradox. The classic example is a statement attributed to Epimenides, and quoted by St. Paul (Titus 1: 12–13) in his advise to a bishop named Titus, whom Paul sent to Crete. According to the King James version, Paul wrote: "One of themselves, even a prophet of their own, said, The Cretans are always liars, evil beasts, slow bellies. This witness is true." As Epimenides himself was a Cretan, his assertion that all statements by Cretans are false could not be true because his own statement would necessarily be encompassed by his claim. This problem has been a topic for logicians, who have generated several competing theories about presuppositions and the relative truth value of sentences.[3] Sacks (1975) addresses a version of this paradox in his examination of the statement "Everyone has to lie." Like Epimenides' statement, this one must be incorporated in its own assertion. Sacks analyzes the paradox by observing that the categorization "everyone" can be taken in three ways: as summatively construed, duplicatively organized, or productively useful.

It is only under the first sense that the paradox exists in its classic form. Everyone as summatively construed includes all "eaches" contained in a category. Hence, if an exception can be found, the statement is false. Everyone as duplicatively organized refers to members of some specified group rather than to the set of all persons. Sacks provides an example taken from a billboard advertisement for a metropolitan newspaper: "It has something for everyone: the news for Dad, the women's page for Mom, the sports page for brother, and the fashion page for sis." Here, "everyone" refers to the categories of the larger membership group, family. The third sense, productively useful, suggests that anyone may eventually find himself in such a situation. Here, "everyone has to lie" is a claim that "everyone" might possibly find occasion to do so but not necessarily that any particular person has. It is in this latter sense that the phrase normally takes its meaning in discourse.

The paradox of the secret also contains an essential contradiction. In telling a secret, the informant, either directly or tacitly, makes the claim that the information he or she speaks is not to be spoken. The respondent is instructed to hear talk and at the same time disclaim that the telling is violating or exposing the secret. In the same way as Sacks's productively useful sense of the category contains metacommunicative instructions for framing the assertion "Everyone has to lie," the preface to the telling of a secret—"Don't tell anyone, but . . ."—contains the metacommunicative instruction to frame the activity of telling as an instance of legitimate informing rather than exposing. In Sacks's terminology, the "anyone" here is duplicatively organized. That is, it refers to specific "anyones" rather than to the entire population. Different cohorts of members can be identified by their respective rights to know. This suggests that social networks can be defined according to access to types of concealed knowledge. The very identification of whether some piece of information is or is not a secret is indirectly a matter of membership identification.

The display of membership that accompanies the keeping and telling of secrets is most observable in the practices of secret societies. It is there that "what is secret" is always a concern of participants. The display of membership is both a way of establishing mutual interests and a way of advancing in rank and power. Through an investigation of a series of rituals of a major West African secret society, the Poro, I have been able to isolate the phenomenon of secrecy for analysis. All men in communities where the Poro exists must belong, as must all women to a sister society, the Sande. These associations occur among the Mande-speaking peoples of Liberia, Sierra Leone, the Ivory Coast, and, today illegally, Guinea. In this book I examine the Poro as it is practiced by the largest cultural group in Liberia, the Kpelle.[4]

Where the Poro is legal, it serves as the primary political and religious entity at the local level. Each community that has the Poro possesses both a sacred and a secular ruling structure. The secular comprises the town chief, the ritual "owner of the land," quarter chiefs from different patri-local compounds, headmen, and respected elders. They mostly are responsible for adjudicating minor torts and adultery cases and for tax collection. The sacred ruling structure is the Zo, or priest hierarchy, of both the Poro and the Sande. They are responsible for adjudicating major disputes including acts of violence, rape, incest as well as serious verbal abuses, land-tenure contests between towns, and traditionally, warfare. Because all men must join the Poro and all women the Sande, a question arises as to what is meant by "secret society" when referring to these associations. The answer one expects is that the secrets of the Poro are those men hold from women, and the secrets of the Sande are those women hold from men. But there is much more.

Within both the Poro and the Sande are a number of other secret societies that meet in concert with the larger associations. There are also several subsidiary groups under the ultimate authority of the Poro and the Sande but which meet separately and in most activities are independent of them. To join these, all prospective members first belong either to the Poro or the Sande. A reason for this is expressed in the Kpelle parable *Porong nuu e kaa goi zu* ('The Poro man is in the stomach'). One interpretation is that, because every man belongs to the Poro, the members of the other secret societies can take for granted that the new initiate already knows how to keep a secret. When a man joins the Poro and a woman the Sande, they learn both how to keep a secret and the consequences of inappropriate exposure. After initiation they are held responsible by the entire adult community for being able to keep a secret.

Before joining the Poro a male cannot take part in any serious discussion where important decisions are made, as he is not considered trustworthy. Likewise, before joining the Sande, a female is under moral constraints not to have sexual relations and is almost totally under the authority of her parents. It is within the initiation rituals that the issue of secrecy becomes a serious matter for participants. Once members of the Poro and the Sande, the new initiates are considered responsible adults. During initiation the instruction in how to keep a secret is conjoined with the responsibility for maintaining it.

Initiation into the Poro begins when the novices are presented by their families to the *kwelebah*, a non-Zo officer of the society, who ties a thatch sash around each of them to signify their new initiate status and that no woman can approach them. The following morning they are taken behind the Poro fence outside of town, where they engage in a mock battle with a member who is masquerading as one of the society's forest spirits (*noi sheng*, literally 'bush things'), or "devils,"[5] called *ngamu*. They are symbolically killed and eaten as marks are incised on their necks, chests, and backs. Each community Poro organization has its own distinctive scarification design. In this way Poro members can determine the particular Poro group an initiate joined. After scarification, the initiates are taken to a specially constructed village in the forest, where they live apart from the women. Both while they are being scarred and later when they are led to the initiation village, the *kwelebah* returns to town, first to announce that the boys were killed by *ngamu* and then to report that they have been successfully "reborn" by the Zo inside the womb of the *ngamu*'s wife.

In the village the initiates practice various crafts, hunt, and learn some basic medicines. This is a period when lifelong extra-kin friendship bonds are established and the boys learn how to survive without having to rely on their mothers and sisters. Most of their daily activities resemble their secular life except that they live under strict discipline and must practice great respect toward their elders and all other members of the society. Their experience is similar in this regard to that of the female initiates of the Sande, who learn how to live separately from the men while they too are secluded in their own initiation village several years after the Poro initiation-ritual process has ended (see Bledsoe, 1980). Those initiates who are the children of Zo and other officers of the society are given special instruction in how to perform the various Poro rituals, which will enable them to take over their fathers' positions in the society after their initiation is finished. In addition, those initiates who demonstrate a particular interest in the internal affairs of the society and who are least likely to leave the community for the modern sector are trained to perform as the different Poro bush-things or devils.

Traditionally, this period of seclusion lasted four years; owing to the costs now involved, most groups have reduced the sessions to one year. Initiates can join at any time during the year. Those who intend eventually to take over the Zo positions and other offices enter at the beginning of the year, whereas students and those coming from the modern sector join near the end. Once a novice enters the process he must remain in the initiation community until completion. When the year is over, the initiates and members make animal sacrifices and eat together in larger feasts within the forest village. Each initiate is given a Poro name with which he will from then on be called, both within the society and in daily life. The initiates are then taken back to the community at a time when all women are forbidden to leave their homes. They then participate in a ritual performance of being symbolically reborn from the womb of another bush-thing called the *ngamu*'s wife. They are then taken to another fence outside of town, where they bathe, have white chalk rubbed on their bodies, and dress in newly sewn gowns given them by their families or sponsors in the society. The next afternoon they are led single file throughout the community and presented to the town chief. After the chief accepts the initiates they are released from the custody of the Poro Zo to their respective families.

In making this study of secrecy through an investigation of the Poro, I used a combination of methods. But constant throughout the entire project, from the first field investigation to the analysis of the last piece of data, was my concern with the participants' or members' perspective. I took the phenomenological approach as my guideline because of its concern with the analysis of the world as perceived rather than with the development of constructs that explain facets of social organization but ignore members' own perceptions of their social realities.[6] Instead of beginning with a deductive theory and generating hypotheses to test it, I employed the abductive approach.[7] That is, I examined my data to locate particular phenomena, and then I developed and tested a theory to account for them.

I started with myriad data obtained from my years of field observation and as a participant in several Kpelle secret societies. Much of this research was conducted in Sucromu, which is renowned for being a center of Poro activity and is the present location of the paramount chief of all Zo, or Poro priest-leaders, for the Kpelle in the area. I first began research there in 1967, remained almost two years, and have returned some twelve times for shorter periods.

I joined secret societies and participated in as many local activities as I was able. Although it may appear curious that a Western social scientist was permitted entry into African secret societies, the ability to join is based more on the ability to find a sponsor in the societies and a willingness to undergo the risks of the initiation rituals than on any other factor. When I first worked in Liberia I was able to gain the confidence of several Kpelle students at Cuttington College who were working for Michael Cole and John Gay. After several months they suggested that I work in Sucromu because of its reputation as a center for secret-society activity. One of these students had several contacts in the community and was himself a member of the Snake Society there. He then sponsored my membership in the society and convinced the Zo, the elders, and the town chief that I be given permission to join and take up residence in the community. After joining the Snake Society the Zo of other secret societies became interested in my joining their associations.

As an observer-participant I kept notes about the social organization and range of issues relevant to the situations I was in. By participating in a number of different social situations, I was able to observe how each was structured. I asked questions using both questionnaires (administered by either myself or trained informant field assistants) and elicitation procedures developed by cognitive scientists to discover the semantic dimensions of various categories. More specifically, I employed a version of the sentence-frame elicitation methodology developed by Metzger (1963) and others; that is, locating the taxonomic structure of some semantic domain by asking questions about what terms can be substituted within a given sentence frame. Mary Black (1969) argues that the best environment in which to ask such questions is a controlled setting, or the so-called white room of the anthropologist's field station. Because I was concerned with how setting and situation worked to structure the taxonomic order of the categories I dealt with, I thus used the elicitation technique in a variety of differing social settings and attended to the consistent ways in which differences in responses occurred.

Essentially I recognized my task to be that of learning the Kpelle language, both *langue* and *parole*. The former, I gained by traditional linguistic field methods supplemented by the structural analysis of Kpelle by Welmers (1948). The latter is an ongoing process, as it involves a knowledge of the rules for using categories in a native-speaker or member-recognized manner. The division, here, is similar also to Chomsky's (1965) classic distinction between competence and performance. I agree with Cicourel (1974) and others who question whether the two can really be separated in practice. In any case, my ongoing task is to develop my performance skills in Kpelle and to formalize those procedures when possible. I observed that the semantic structure of many categories depended on the type of social reality that provided the auspices for each situation. Consequently, my interest goes beyond the taxonomic description of Kpelle terms to the analysis of how collections of categories are applied in discourse.[8]

In addition to asking questions, I also video- and audio-recorded as many social interactions, palavers, and secret-society rituals as possible. Along with a team of Kpelle field assistants, I would place a number of audio recorders in and around the area of an activity. When possible, other informant assistants would video-record what was occurring. Very often, because of my own membership in several of the secret societies, I was able to be near the center of activity. Later, I would replay the video- and audiotapes to my informants and the other principals involved in the recorded event to obtain their narrative accounts. The analysis of what they recalled, its order, and what they placed as central and peripheral provided additional materials for understanding their perception and interpretation of the recorded events.[9]

When I returned from the field, I worked closely with my Kpelle assistants in this country to transcribe, transliterate, and finally translate the recorded data. In addition, I developed a method for analyzing each videotape by attending to the systematic use of particular in-camera editing procedures that each informant cameraperson used. I found that the format of each recorded tape provided an access for understanding content. Thus, the study of the cameraperson's selective attention during the recording process provided a method for describing the recorded event from the native speaker's perspective.[10]

My analyses of the transcripts presented are based in part on my many years of research, which have enabled me to gain access to the historicity of events that constitutes the background knowledge necessary to interpret the meanings that are contained in them. The process of translation used was, first, for me to view the video recordings and listen to the Kpelle audiotapes alone, then with my Kpelle research assistants. Next we transliterated each string of talk and provided a translation. I recorded our discussions and debates about the subtle meaning shifts that occurred and then incorporated the results of those discussions in final translations.

As Gadamer (1975) points out, "Every translation is at the same time an interpretation" (p. 346), as is also the case with understanding. For Gadamer, "All understanding is interpretation, and all interpretation takes place in the medium of a language which would allow the object to come into words and yet is at the same time the interpreter's own language" (p. 350). In the case of the transcripts presented in this book, I have accepted in most instances the language of my research assistants in translating from Kpelle into English, then verified these interpretations by subsequent visits to the field in which I discussed our analyses with the principals involved in the initiation rituals and other events described here. Thus, the interpretation of the "deep talk" and the ritual metaphors and symbols is based on those interviews as well as on the advise of my assistants. In most cases there was general agreement about the meaning of a passage. In cases where there were divergent interpretations or alternate meanings possible, I used my own judgment, as based on my years of research in the communities involved. The transcripts are, therefore, presented in the words of my assistants, which is in the Liberian dialect of English. Because there are several passages that may be difficult for the reader to understand, I have paraphrased or explained their meanings in brackets where necessary.

2
The Poro
in West Africa

Secret societies have been a part of African social and political life for centuries. After independence, however, many nations declared them illegal.[1] In other countries, secret societies continue to flourish and often function as a major and legitimate force in local-level politics. Many of these groups cut across ethnic, language, and national boundaries. The Poro is geographically the largest such association in West Africa. It is practiced in Sierra Leone, Liberia, the Ivory Coast, and (today, illegally) Guinea. Because the society has had to respond to different attitudes toward its existence, the Poro is a resource for understanding how secret associations operate and are able to accommodate different social, political, and historical conditions.

The Poro and Sande are the most important local-level secret associations in Liberia. This is due in part to the governmental policy, established under the regime of President W. V. S. Tubman (1944–1971), of incorporating the Poro by placing it under the authority of the Ministry of Local Government. Secret societies are practiced throughout Liberia, even among the smaller ethnic groups that do not have the Poro and Sande. One of these smaller groups, the so-called Americo-Liberians, or descendants of the black settler families that came to Liberia from the United States and Barbados, organized the Masons and the United Brotherhood Fellowship (UBF) as secret societies. They identified with other Masonic groups in West Africa and with black Freemasonry in the United States.[2] Although these societies were organized and controlled by the Americo-Liberians, economically successful ethnic elites were permitted membership.

After Tubman succeeded to the presidency he joined the Poro and declared himself "Grand-Zo" for the Poro throughout Liberia. When

13

Tubman died, William Tolbert became both president and Grand-Zo. This led many other Americo-Liberian elite to join the society. In areas where they joined, they established local chapters of the UBF to initiate ethnic elites. In many places, especially areas where Americo-Liberians had farms or other business interests, membership in the UBF was considered equivalent to membership in the Spirit Society, the secret society that functions as a liaison between the Poro and the Sande.

This relationship between the Poro and the Americo-Liberian government was affected by the Liberian coup of April 14, 1980. Most of those who conspired to overthrow the Tolbert regime were from ethnic groups that did not have the Poro. The majority of the members of the revolutionary government, the Peoples' Redemption Council, are from the southwestern part of the country, which has very little Poro activity. The Tolbert government had taken little interest in developing that part of Liberia inasmuch as the best farming and mining lands were in the other sections where the Poro was practiced. After the revolution, several of the Americo-Liberian members of the Tolbert government attempted to use their relationship to the Poro network of communities to escape the country. Although those who cooperated with such efforts were punished, the government has not established a formal policy against Poro, which continues to function under the authority of the Ministry of Local Government as an important part of local government.

The Poro is also an important secret association at the local level among many Mande-speaking peoples in Sierra Leone (Harris and Sawyer, 1968; Little, 1965; McCormack 1978, 1979) where, in the rural areas, the Poro and Sande function similarly to their counterparts in Liberia. In the modern sector, the society has become something analogous to a workers union or association (Little, 1966a). Its members discuss problems and working conditions under the security of the Poro's secrecy proscription. Although in Liberia the Poro has not developed into such a unionlike association, its members in the modern sector often refer to their membership as a way of insuring the confidentiality of discussions, particularly about serious matters that have occurred in their interior home communities. This reference to mutual Poro membership has the effect of distinguishing first-generation migrants from members of the same social class in both the urban and periurban areas. The fact that the Liberian government incorporated the Poro under its administrative authority explains in part why the Poro in Liberia is not normally used as a worker's advocacy group.

The significance of the Poro is also evident in the southern part of Guinea, where it is now illegal. That area is considered by many Liberian Kpelle and Loma to be where the society first originated. When Guinea became independent of France, President Sékou Touré outlawed the

Poro but permitted the practice of the Sande and various Poro subsidiary associations such as the Horn (or Witch-beating) Society, the Spirit Society, the Iron Society, the Snake Society, the Lightning Society, and other localized secret medicine groups. The Poro was declared illegal, not because it was a secret society, but because of its importance as a principal political organization at the community level. Members of the Touré government, being mostly Moslem and Mandingo, excluded themselves from joining the Poro, citing the Koranic law that forbade their entry into any non-Islamic association. Thus, in contrast to Liberian incorporation of the Poro as part of the administrative apparatus at the local-government level, Guinea treated it as competition to its rule.

Even though the Poro is illegal in Guinea, it remains an active and important association in the areas where it was formerly practiced openly. Traditionally, new members are initiated into the society every sixteen-to-eighteen years in a cycle corresponding to the Sande initiation period. Since the Poro was outlawed, the Guineans have sent their novices to Liberia to join. During the last initiations, more than 50 percent of those joining in communities adjacent to the Liberia-Guinea border were migrants from Guinea. Many had to come illegally across the border through bush paths at night. There was an especially large influx during the final months of the bush-school session, but many came at the beginning of the initiation period and remained in the bush for the entire year. After the final rituals in which the initiates were given their new names, most returned to Guinea to participate in an underground version of the society. Many of those who remained asserted that they eventually would go back to Guinea after working for a period in Liberia to repay their Liberian sponsors for the costs of their initiations.

The Poro and Sande are also present in parts of the Ivory Coast, but there is some question about their relationship to these societies as practiced in Liberia, Sierra Leone, and Guinea. According to Fischer (1980), the Dan in Liberia and the Ivory Coast and the northern Mano in Liberia have masked secret societies that have been confused with the Poro. He claims that these societies are really circumcision-ritual groups that use masks that only resemble the Poro bush-things. The terms *Poro* and *Sande* (or *Sandogo* among the Senufo) are actually used for the men's and women's societies among the Senufo and northern Baule (Glaze, 1975; Goldwater, 1964); yet these societies differ in many respects from their counterparts in Liberia, Sierra Leone, and Guinea. First, there is a much closer relationship between the two societies in ritual activities in that women are permitted access to many Poro masked-ritual performances. Second, because most communities represent a large mixture of Islamic and Poro peoples, the society does not play as dominant a role in local governance as it does in the other Poro areas. The Poro and Sande are primarily used to initiate young men and women into adulthood and to provide the membership with medicine protections against malefic spirits, witchcraft, and the negative forces of nature. Finally, the societies have developed an extensive artistic tradition in weaving and the carving of bone, wood, and stone that is independent of the Poro arts in the other countries. Although there may be some historical connections to the other Poro and Sande societies, the Poro and Sande in the Ivory Coast are today isolated from the major areas of Poro activity, causing independent traditions to develop.

The Poro in Liberia, Sierra Leone, Guinea, and the Ivory Coast have adapted to each country's respective social and political conditions. Yet, the basic structure and importance of the society remains, whether it has been incorporated into the political system as in Liberia, exists alongside that system as in Sierra Leone, has accommodated itself to governmental policies against it by becoming an underground association as in Guinea, or coexists with non-Poro religious and political structures at the local level as a method for institutionalizing culture identity as in the Ivory Coast.

Previous ethnographic accounts of the Poro and related societies described the sequential order of ritual events (Bellman, 1975; Harley, 1941a, 1941b, 1950; Welmers, 1949), the meanings of the masks and other ritual paraphernalia (Adams, 1980; Bellman, 1975; d'Azevedo, 1965, 1973a, 1973b; Harley, 1950; Siegmann and Schmidt, 1977), and the relationship of the Poro to both the public, or secular, ruling structure of the community and the other voluntary secret associations (Adams, 1980; Bellman, 1975, 1979; Bledsoe, 1980; Cole, Gay, Glick and Sharp, 1971; Erchack, 1977; Fulton, 1972; Gay, 1973; Harley, 1941a, 1941b, 1950; McCormack, 1979; Murphey, 1976). Although there is much descriptive detail contained in each of these studies, seldom are the authors clear as to what constitutes the real secrets of the Poro. Even Harley, who was the first to write extensively on the Poro, did not formally consider such early Mano practices as human sacrifice and ritual cannibalism to be secrets.[3] He did, however, frequently use the term *secret* in his books and admitted that the information he described was for "untold generations guarded information." Harley assumed, because he as an outsider to the Poro was able to gain access to concealed information, that the society as an institution must be breaking down. Decades after Harley collected his data on the society and in spite of his negative prognosis for its future and his claim that the secrets were no longer as guarded as before, the Poro continues. Besides saying much about the tenacity of the association, this suggests that the information Harley considered so secret was not really crucial to the Poro's longevity and purpose as a secret society. Hence, the corpus of secrets belonging to the society cannot be as stable as he assumed. Instead, "what must not be talked" has been adapted to the political conditions and policies of the countries where the Poro is practiced. The *contents* of the secrets are not as significant as are the *doing* of secrecy and the recognition that a do-not-talk-it proscription is a feature of all legitimate social interactions.

Some may argue that, because the Poro today is under the authority of different federal goverments and no longer has the power to declare open warfare, the society is on the decline. The Poro has been mentioned in various written records going back more than four hundred years. Many of those descriptions are travelers' accounts that tend to confuse any masked secret-society activity with Poro activity. Yet, there are also descriptions that most probably are of legitimate Poro activities. During this extensive period of recorded history there has been much political upheaval and social change. Rather than assume that the Poro has remained the same and only recently undergone change, it is more reasonable to look at the tenacity of the society as evidence for its general ability to adapt to different social environments and political situations. The ability of the society to adapt is particularly evident in the Liberian community of Kpaiyea,where the town operates two separate Poro organizations. The existence of this dual Poro structure within the same community suggests that organizational features may change without significantly affecting the integrity of the association.

Although the Poro is very important, it is not universally practiced throughout the culture area. In the Ivory Coast, the Poro has the same political status as many other coexisting voluntary secret associations; whereas, in those communities that have the Poro in Liberia, Sierra Leone, and Guinea, all non-Poro associations are under the ultimate authority of the society. In those communities where the Poro does not exist, many nonrelated secret societies have borrowed Poro symbols and incorporated some of its ritual practices into their associations. Poro members are easily able to identify those practices as different from their uses in their society. In the following chapter I discuss the Poro and a number of other secret societies as practiced in Kpelle communities along the Liberia-Guinea border. Because I accept the theoretical premise that social structure is an accomplished phenomenon, my discussion of social structure is documented with case histories and analyses of social interactions to demonstrate the methods used for that accomplishment.

Most descriptions of the Poro are more concerned with what the society was like in the past than with analyzing its current structure and organization. Even Harley (1941b, 1950) claimed that his detailed and extensive discussion of the Poro was really a reconstruction. What I find remarkable is that the society continues to exist and maintain great power at the local level in spite of the rapid modernization that has occurred throughout the culture area. Consequently, this discussion is of the Poro mostly as it exists in contemporary society. I have treated informant descriptions about what the society may have been like in the past as intentional communications relating to the present practices of the society. As Schutz and Luckmann (1973) maintain, historicizations all "originate from socially conditioned motives" (p. 284). The significance of history is found mostly in how it is recognized by practitioners and manifested in current practices. References to ancestors, say Schutz and Luckmann, involve "because" motives ("We do as we do today because our ancestors did it"), whereas accounts of cultural degeneration are intentionally motivated. Cultures do not degenerate; they only change. An assertion that some practice has degenerated is a value-laden assessment of what is happening in the present. Instead of being descriptive, it is judgmental.

3
The Poro and Other Secret Societies in the Vavala Clan

A description of the Poro cannot be a general characterization of the society because significant structural differences exist between Poro societies even within the same language group or tribe. Many Kpelle consider the Poro practiced by the Mano, Vai, and Gola to be quite distinct from their own. They recognize a communality of membership depending on the interactional context rather than on the fact of belonging to the same association. For example, a Mano male visiting a Fala Kpelle community would not have to enter a house when the devil is performing, as would a nonmember. He may, however, be restricted from entering the Zo house or certain areas within a devil fence and from participating in the discussion or matter that served as the reason for the devil's appearance in the community. On the other hand, if a Loma or Gbande man should visit, he will have much more access to the societal meetings, discussions, and rituals.

My discussion of the Poro is as practiced by the Fala Kpelle of the Vavala clan in Lofa county. Most of the materials presented in this book are from the Poro and the related societies in Sucromu (see map), which is the headquarters for the Poro for all Kpelle speakers in the entire country. It is the home of the paramount chief of all Zo for the Kpelle peoples in the county and shares a reputation with the Loma community of Malawu for being a town reputed for its secret societies and powerful medicines. The town is comprised of 218 dwellings with a population of about fifteen hundred people. It has twelve active secret associations and occasionally, depending on the residency of certain Zo, can have up to fifteen separate societies being practiced. I also describe a second community, Kpaiyea. Through a comparison of these two Fala Kpelle towns, I analyze how the structure of the society can vary yet at the same time be recognized across commmunities.

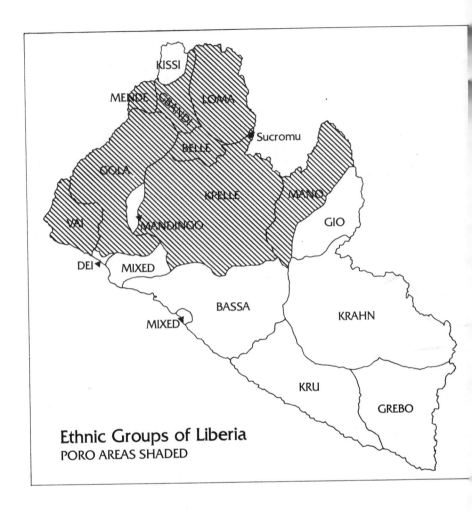

Ethnic Groups of Liberia
PORO AREAS SHADED

Sucromu: An Ethnographic Sketch

Originally, Sucromu was two towns, Sucronsu and Twasamu, that joined together during wars with the Loma. Each town is named after a sacred mountain and maintains its separate identity as a moiety by having its own food taboo, or *tinya*, and by making sacrifices to its mountain. The people of Sucromu maintain that when a man dies, his spirit goes to the mountain of his ancestors, where he joins them in a patrilineally organized spirit village that parallels the social organization of the living community. The two towns, or *taai*, are in a mother's brother–sister's son (*ngala-maling*) relation to one another. Sucronsu is *ngala* (mother's brother) to Twasamu and is where the Poro and most of its major support in secret societies are located. Twasamu, on the other hand, traditionally has selected the town chief and is the home of the family known as the "owner of the land," or *loi kalong* (literally 'land chief' but translated into Liberian English as "landlord"). Although the Poro society is autonomous in its powers, it must first obtain the ritual permission of the *loi kalong* before it can hold its initiation rituals.[1] In that sense, the position of landlord is considered above that of the Zo; in practice, however, the Poro is responsible for protecting the town and for adjudicating serious matters.

Both of the *taai*, Sucronsu and Twasamu, are divided into patrilocal compounds, or quarters, called *kolii*. Each *koli* comprises a patrilineage ruled over by its senior male as quarter chief (*koli kalong*) along with various respected elders. The quarters are strictly exogamous. Because there are *tinya* for each *taa*, as well as for each *koli*, the recitation of food taboos is often a way of determining one's kinship relationships. The *kolii*, like the *taai*, are in a *ngala-maling* relation to each other. Consequently, the members of the respective *kolii* have formally recognized rights and obligations toward one another, and as all the *kolii* in Twasamu are *maling* to those in Sucronsu, the members of the latter *taa* exercise ritual political authority during both quarter and moiety interactions.

Although residence is patrilocal, many live with their mother's family or *ngala*. This practice is especially common when one's father has not paid full dowry or bride-price for the mother. There are several types of domestic situations ranging from a formally recognized love relationship to full marriage, which involves (1) either the payment in full of forty dollars in bride-price or partial payments, tokens, or both given to the woman's family; (2) the payment of costs for special sacrifices for a pregnancy; and (3) the protection of the child before being weaned.[2] Divorce and separation are common except where full bride-price has been paid. When separations occur, the woman often returns to her family's *koli* accompanied by her children. As the children grow older, they work for her brother (their *ngala*) instead of their father. Persons who live in this latter arrangement are subordinate to the patrilocal residents of the *koli* and do not participate in their yearly sacrifices on the sacred mountain (Suckalaw for residents of Sucronsu moiety, and Twasa for residents of Twasamu).

One of the *kolii*, Zoman of Sucronsu *taa*, is the patrilineage from which the Poro Zo hierarchy are recruited. Its members claim to have come from Guinea and to be one family (*kala tano*) with the Poro Zo quarters in other towns throughout the district, whether they be Kpelle or Loma. They do not always recognize kinship with Poro Zo from more distant groups, however, even speakers of other Kpelle dialects. One segment of Zo live outside of Zoman *koli* in Yamii *koli*, the patrilocal compound where the Poro fence is located. This quarter, like all the others in town, is divided into subquarters. Yamii is divided first into a lower and an upper half, as the *koli* sits on a small hill. It is in this lower part, in an area named after a famous and powerful Zo ancestor, Bobo, that the Zo reside. Residents of this subquarter refer to the area as Bobo *koli*. They consider themselves to be the *maling*, or sister's child, of the other Yamii subquarter residents. One of the other subquarters also is a Zo family related to Bobo in the *ngala-maling* relationship. They refer to their subquarter by the name of their quarter chief, Kpokawlaw, who is a major Poro Zo. He is responsible for maintaining the outside gate to the Poro fence that surrounds the Zo house where internal Poro discussions and palavers are held. Because the *maling* is expected to show deference to the *ngala*, the other Poro Zo always pay him formal respect, and all Poro matters are "reached" to him before entering into a palaver or engaging in ritual activity.[3]

Thus there are two ways of reckoning the *ngala-maling* relationship: (1) that defined by actual descent and (2) the symbolic relationship of the different patrilocal quarters and moieties to each other. In either case, the *maling* is expected to show deference to the *ngala*. This is expressed through a number of formal rights and obligations that each has toward the other. During rituals and sacrifices, these rights and duties are especially important. For example, whenever a cow is sacrificed, the *ngala* is given the head and the *maling* the tail.[4] Also, during the Poro initiations, the *maling* always presents his initiated sons to the *ngala* for approval both before they enter the initiation fence and after they are returned to the community after their period of seclusion. The *maling* of the Zo, the *kwelebah*, is one of the most important non-Zo offices in the society and is especially active during the initiation-ritual process.

Besides the serious or formal rights and obligations between *ngala* and *maling*, other aspects of the relationship are expressed as joking behavior between kinsmen. When drinking palm wine, the *maling* is "to take off the dirt" by taking the first drink, whereas the *ngala* gets the last dregs from the bottom of the gourd; the *maling* is permitted to take any of the *ngala*'s clothes without asking, while the *ngala* can take the *maling*'s hat; and where there are not enough seats available, the *maling* will stand and offer the chair to his *ngala*. The *ngala-maling* relationship is also the basis for labor recruitment, financial assistance, and a general support network. During disputes, the relationship can be evoked as a way to play down the seriousness of the matter, as can be seen in a palaver presented in Chapter 5. In the transcript, Muwulu was speaking and was interrupted by Kokulah. Muwulu threatened his interrupter. The latter then used his *maling* status to institute a repair. Thus, the mutual recognition of this relationship is significant to virtually every aspect of life, from the most formal rituals to frivolous interaction.

The Kpelle recognize a preferential marriage within the *ngala-maling* relationship. Although it is forbidden for a person to marry his or her own mother's brother's child, both are considered to be in a play (*kpili*) relationship. A man may thus ask his mother's brother's daughter to cook or work for him as he would a wife, and he is also permitted to have limited sexual play with her short of actual intercourse. When this woman marries, her husband must give a small tribute payment to his wife's *ngala* because, as several of my informants have related, "he [the *ngala*] is the husband of the woman." The child from her marriage or the child of her brother can, and is often encouraged to, marry the *ngala* or one of his children. In this manner the *ngala-maling* relationship can shift in alternate generations.

Just as each of the quarters is related to the others through the *ngala-maling* relationship, Sucromu residents also categorize other Kpelle communities with this system. This is especially true of those towns in Guinea that are immediately on the other side of the border. In the Poro initiations this is significant and is symbolically expressed in the formal rhetoric used when the initiates are presented to the community by the Zo leadership. Because the Poro is considered to have originated in Guinea, the people from there are considered the *ngala*. The special deference shown to the Guinea visitors during the Poro rituals is expressed solely in terms of the *ngala-maling* interaction. It represents a structural dichotomy as important as the differentiation between the sacred and secular division within the community.

The relationship between the Zo and the rest of Sucromu is also expressed through the *ngala-maling* relation. I mentioned above that the presence of the Zo family in Yamii *koli* is an instance of a *maling* coming to live with the *ngala*, a typical pattern of avunculocal residence. This pattern is reversed, however, when during ritual activities, certain members of Yamii are called the *maling*. When this claim is made, the Zo family differentiates itself from the entire Sucronsu moiety and is considered to be a separate enclave of its own. In an interview with the senior elder and Zo from Bobo *koli*, Mulbahzuah, he told me that originally his family (the residents of Bobo in Yamii *koli*, and most of those living in Zoman *koli*) came from a different town called Palapulu. It was only after Twasamu and Sucronsu joined together that his group became part of the latter *taa*. In fact, Mulbahzuah claimed that the Zo family payed hut taxes for the houses in Palapulu up until the recent abolition of such taxes by the postrevolutionary Liberian government in 1981. That area is now Bobo *koli*'s farming village. Thus, although it is really part of Sucromu territory, it legally had the status, under the previous government of Liberia, of a separate town. The Zo family, having come from Guinea and settled in the Vavala area, can be considered the *ngala*. Yet, because they are now a part of Sucronsu *taa*, they assume a *maling* relation to the other Yamii *koli* residents.

The shift in the use of the *ngala* and *maling* terms is often the topic of joking between friends. This is exemplified in the relationship between Folpahzoi, who is a Zo member of Bobo, and Walawulu, who is Kpokawlaw's eldest son and Zo of the Baiyaemu society.[5] Although Folpahzoi is a Zo, he was, during the period of the last Poro initiations, the legal town chief. When the former chief, Bakollee Volpoi, announced his retirement and the previous chief, Vallai, did not want to resume the office, the town elders met and asked Folpahzoi to take the office. Rather than merge the sacred and secular ruling structures, Folpahzoi announced that he was not going to take an active part in Poro activities, while he was the chief. Folpahzoi and Walawulu had joined the Poro together about thirty-five years before and since that time been close friends, a bond expressed through the *ngala-maling* joking relationship.

When Folpahzoi and Walawulu interact, they use the relationship to locate their informal rights within the setting. Although each can be *ngala* or *maling* depending on the technique of reckoning, each argues that he is the *maling* to the other. By making the other *ngala*, the speaker is entitled to take the first drink of palm wine or cane juice (raw rum) and can even take wine from the other's palm tree without permission. As the *maling*, the claimant can also jokingly abuse the other and use his status as a way of avoiding any retribution. I have recorded several hours of their ongoing speech play, especially during those occasions when one has a large gourd of palm wine to share.[6] On the other hand, whenever there is Poro activity or official family business between their respective subcompounds of Yamii *koli*, both men take their formal structural positions without any debate. Their relationship is only problematic, and thus subject to the joking behavior, during the secular social realities.

The Representative Powers of Poro

The sacred ruling is headed by the Zo hierarchy of the Poro society. The Zo are ranked according to their responsibilities during the initiation rituals. Together, the hierarchy constitutes a thirteen-man priesthood structured in a rank order that varies according to the type of ritual the group performs. Their offices include the Zo *nang* ("father"), who both represents the priesthood and acts as their liaison with the townspeople; a Zo to whom all initiates (*kpulu nuu*) are brought before entering the initiation bush village; the several Zo who are in charge of the different devils or bush-things; the keeper of the door to the Zo house, who is responsible for protecting the dwelling from intruders; the keeper of the gate to the fence in front of the Zo house; different Zo who are responsible for the various categories of initiates and their respective training while they are living in the bush-school initiation village; a Zo who is responsible for disciplining the members; and a Zo who adjudicates any disputes between members of the Zo hierarchy as well as any that occur between the various secret societies subsidiary to the Poro and under its administrative authority. One of the Zo has the additional responsibility of serving as the government, or *kwii*, Zo. Whenever the Ministry of Local Government wants to communicate information to a local Poro association, this Zo is contacted. Such messages might involve the collection of special taxes, announce that a high-level government official is going to pass through the area and that the dancing devil of the society should perform, or give permission for performing the initiation rituals of the society.

The Zo ranking in any given situation depends on the ritual or business (*meni*) that is the purpose of their gathering. Although the organizational basis for the interaction is Poro *meni*, there are a variety of inclusive matters that members also refer to as the *meni* for the situation. These include the making of sacrifices, the preparation of special societal medicines, the adjudication of disputes, the presentation of initiates to the *loi kalong*, interactions with Zo from different communities, and the performance of the various society devils.

The shift in Zo ranking is best exemplified in the case of the Zo *nang*. As the liaison between the townspeople and the *loi kalong* on the one hand and the hierarchy on the other, he is sometimes considered to be the first Zo in the rankings. This is demonstrated on those occasions when he leads the other Zo in a procession throughout the town. On occasions when there is no direct interaction with the townspeople (e.g., when the devils perform in the town), the Zo *nang* stands either to the rear or to the side of the Zo procession. When he is at the rear he is considered to be the last Zo ranked; when he is to the side, he is considered to be tangential to the hierarchy. Whenever the Zo gather there are always servings of food and drink. The amount and order in which each is served directly relates to the ranking of the member. Thus, depending on the suborder *meni*, the Zo *nang* receives different proportions and orders of service.

The Poro society, as the sacred political structure, is concerned with in-town fighting, murder, rape, the violation of a girl before puberty, land-tenure disputes between towns, and the breaking of major laws of the medicines. Prior to government control, before two towns would enter into open warfare, the palaver was discussed by members of the respective Poro leadership of each community. Then the *ngamu*, or devils, of each town would engage in a mock battle. If the *ngamu* of one was victorious, the other community would capitulate. Today such matters are still discussed in this way even though overt warfare is now legally prohibited.

Over the years that I have conducted ethnographic work in the Vavala area, there were two occasions where such devil battles occurred. Each of the cases involved the Loma town of Malawu, which is approximately two hours' walk from Sucromu. Malawu is considered to be a major Poro center and Zo community. The Malawu Zo house many special medicines that serve the Poro organizations of nearby towns. In addition, after the government of Liberia established political control over the area and incorporated the Poro under the Ministry of Local Government, Malawu was proclaimed the principal Poro town for the Loma. One of the Zo from that town, Zezeh, is called the *da* Zo, or "head" Zo, for the area. The paramount chief of Kpelle Zo, who resides in Sucromu, and his parallel for the Loma both report to Zezeh. He then directly makes his reports to the ministry. It is important to distinguish between the line of authority established by the central government and that which pertains at the local level. Although the Zo of the Sucromu Poro recognize the Malawu Zo's legal authority over them, they do not consider that the Malawu Zo association dominates. It was over this issue that the two *ngamu* had their battle.

Malawu is situated on top of a large hill that overlooks the entire area. Because it is a difficult climb to reach, it was considered an appropriate place to store special medicines whose laws could easily be broken once the motor road was put through the area in 1959. When one visits Malawu there are special rules that must be obeyed. No one may wear glasses, shoes, or slippers within the town limits. Women must either go bare breasted or wear only their *lappa*s (a wraparound cloth used as a skirt) lifted over their chests. No one can say "The sun is hot" even if the day is especially warm and humid, and no one can pick his teeth with a piece of thatch from a hut. Also, strangers are not given free access to walk about the community. In spite of these rigid rules, there is a high proportion of zinc-roofed houses and many other objects associated with modernity. The rules relate to special medicine objects rather than act as a denial of the modern world. All such objects have particular laws that must be obeyed. In fact, many of the so-called laws of the community are really laws of the medicine. These include those rules against killing, fighting, rape, and incest. Infractions are punished by the Poro as violations of medicine laws. The violation endangers the medicine's ability to protect and thus places the entire community at risk.

Not one in the area doubts Malawu's importance and powers with medicines. All other towns in the area show special respect and deference to its Zo. During my initial field visit to the area, there was a test of power between Malawu and a neighboring Loma community, Killiwu, about thirty minutes' walk away. Because of the closeness of the towns to one another, Killiwu agreed to allow the residents of Malawu to farm on part of its land. In return, the citizens of Killiwu were able to have Malawu's protection as a Zo town. In 1967 the towns had a dispute. The leaders of Killiwu said that, inasmuch as Malawu was using their farmlands, Malawu should be responsible for clearing the farm paths in that area. Malawu argued that, if they cleaned the paths, they would then consider the land to be legally theirs.

Because the dispute concerned land tenure it was a Poro matter. The Zo and other members of the respective Poro associations met at the boundary between the two towns. The devils from each town then came and danced before representatives of the other town. After performing, the Malawu devil held up its arms, and the Killiwu devil ceased to move. At that, the Killiwu leaders apologized to the Malawu Zo and sacrificed a cow for them. According to my informant research assistant, the Killiwu Zo knew that, because their devil had powers based primarily on their medicines, they could not win any dispute against Malawu which was based in Poro *meni*. Although the dispute was first heard and decided inside the devil fence, this ritual was the public enactment of the decision reached.

Around that same time, the Malawu devil also challenged Sucromu, but with a different outcome. The Malawu Zo claimed that all Zo in the area are *kala tano*; therefore they should be able to farm on any land owned by the Sucromu Zo family. The Sucromu Zo, of course, strongly objected. The dispute was enacted before the entire town. One morning the Malawu Zo leadership all appeared in Sucromu and built a small thatch devil fence in front of the Sucromu devil fence. Later in the day, their *ngamu* came out and danced throughout the town. When it came

before the Sucromu fence, it sat down and announced through its interpreter (the *kwelebah*, who is considered *maling* to and servant to the Zo)
that the Sucromu devil or any other devil must not approach it. Should
one appear, it would immediately become paralyzed. Then, the Sucromu
devil appeared in town and danced throughout all the *kolii*. When it
finally came before the seated Malawu *ngamu*, it danced circles around it
and then returned to its fence. The Malawu devil then got up and left
town with its Zo. Hence, neither devil capitulated to the other. Whereas
Killiwu recognized both the legal and actual authority of the Malawu
association over it, Sucromu held onto the integrity and independence of
its own society.

These cases illustrate how the Poro operates as the corporate representative of the larger community. Although the Poro is not really a
military association, it historically provided protection and offensive
medicines to warriors and was the mechanism for military and treaty talks
between towns. It functioned both to establish alliances and to provide an
environment for making military plans under the confidentiality of its
secrecy proscription. The actual military organization was under the
authority of a war chief (*koi kalong*) and various military leaders called
kawlulah. They were part of the secular ruling structure in the same way
as the *loi kalong*. These leaders, nevertheless, recognized the authority of
the Poro for declaring war and making peace. Today, as evidenced in the
cases just discussed, the Poro remains the primary mechanism for intra-
community negotiations.

In addition to the Poro Zo there are also numerous Zo of other secret
societies who also own medicines that allegedly have strong offensive and
protective powers. Whenever the community is threatened, they offer
those medicines to the Poro, who in turn, through their own medicines,
are able to cause all the medicines to work in concert with one another
and operate as a single force called *kai*. The *ngamu* of each community is
the personification of this *kai*. When a *ngamu* from one community stops
the *ngamu* of another, as in the case of the Killiwu-Malawu dispute, the
act is a symbolic expression of the fact that the community represented by
the defeated devil would lose in any altercation between them. On the
other hand, when neither devil stops the other, warfare may result. This
occurred in the Sucromu-Malawu dispute. After the Malawu *ngamu* left
Sucromu, one of the head Sucromu Zo died. A Malawu Zo took responsibility for the death. Shortly thereafter, an important Malawu Zo died,
and a Sucromu Zo took the credit. Afterward, the towns established a
truce that recognized Sucromu's right to its own farmlands. The formal
rituals that the Poro societies perform thus symbolize the social, economic, and political relationships of communities to each other. The Poro
in such instances represents the entire community.

Other Societies in the Poro Complex

There are twelve secret societies in Sucromu, including the Poro and the Sande. Three of these societies are internal to the Poro and can actually be considered part of the association rather than subsidiary to it. Several of my informants referred to this distinction as that between societies that "lay inside of" (*lalaa*) and those that did not (*fe lalaa ni*). The leaders, or Zo, of the so-called *lalaa* societies are recruited from specific families within the Zo patrilineage who are either the residents of Zoman *koli* or the Bobo subquarter of Yamii. To become a Zo of the *fe lalaa ni* societies requires only the volitive act of purchasing the *ngang sale*, or "head of the medicine." Each of the three *lalaa* societies is named for the *noi sheng* or type of *ngamu* that it controls. These society performers are called *noi sheng*, or bush-things, because they represent the collective medicine powers of the Zo. These spirits are said to reside in the forest and come into the community only at the request of the societal leaders.

The highest of these societies is called the *βalasilangamu*, or Sheephorn Devil Society. This society is composed of the entire Poro Zo leadership and other important persons who, in the words of the society's crier, "know themselves" and "put their whole interest in the medicines." It is called together only for the most important of medicine matters and upon the death of its members. The devil is not really masked. Rather, it is similar to two other nonmasked devils discussed below in that the society members purposefully create an auditory illusion that corresponds to a nonmember's account of the phenomenon. Such rituals of illusion are discussed later as they pertain to the initiation of new members and the conveying of concealed knowledge to them. The sounds associated with this *noi sheng* are produced by blowing into a sheep's horn; hence, this devil's name. The horn is designed so that a unique sound is produced. All nonmembers immediately go into their houses when they hear it, just as nonmembers are required to do for the more common *ngamu*, *Ngwalapiye* (see below). Should a nonmember accidentally witness this devil or the society's activities while the town is closed, he allegedly will either die, become blind, or suffer leprosy. People join this society only after they have gained status and success within the community. The costs of joining are quite expensive. Thus, many who could join choose not to do so. Usually only those who are active in the medicine affairs of the other societies are motivated to belong.

The second *lalaa* society is the association into which all men are initiated when they join the Poro. It is normally referred to with the general name of *ngamu* but is also occasionally called *Ngwalapiye* during internal societal discussions. Membership is restricted to males except for one woman called the *tipinenu*. Initiation generally involves the *kpulu nuu*, also called *sina* (after the English "sinner"), or nonmember, being ritually and symbolically killed, undergoing scarification, living in an age-set community, and then being brought back to life by the naming-rebirth and the coming-out rituals discussed later. These events occur only once each generation, about every sixteen-to-eighteen years. Sucromu ended theirs on January 23, 1978. The other towns in the Vavala clan completed theirs during the week before Sucromu did. The leaders of this society are the Poro hierarchy from Zoman.

In addition to the leaders, there are several people who serve the Zo but are not members of the Zo patrilineage. One is the *kwelebah* (*maling* to the Zo), who acts as the messenger between the Zo and townspeople; the capturer of the *kpulu nuu* and the one who leads them into their mock battle with the devil; and also the translator for the *Ngwalapiye* and the controller of the dancing devil (see below). Another non-Zo Poro leader is the *ngamu nea tua nuu*, who carries a staff for the *ngamu* and leads it about the community. Then there is the *Folpah*, or first initiate to join the society and the first to come into the town in the very elaborate coming-out rituals. Finally, there is the woman member of the society, called the *tipinenu*. She is responsible for cooking for the Zo and for preparing the sacrifices that the Zo make. According to Harley (1941b), this woman leader was also responsible for dealing out the death penalty. Her tap on the subject's head with a small object in the shape of an axe was immediately followed by the executioner's blow. Such executions are no longer prevalent. Thus, the *tipinenu* has the primary function in the contemporary Poro of nonsexual wife to the Zo. Her importance, however, is not diminished. She must always be addressed as a male and is referred to by the male name of Folpah.

There are also those who play the parts of *Ngwalapiye* and the various other devils or bush-things. They are not necessarily Zo, as the literature on the Poro suggests, and their identities are known to the adult members of the society. In Sucromu, the player of the *Ngwalapiye* lives in Gbanya *koli*, which is situated between Zoman and Yamii, whereas the main dancing-devil player is the second son of a Zo who resides in Zoman. Both were selected for these parts on talent rather than inherited duty to perform in the roles. Although their identities are known, it is forbidden to discuss that knowledge publicly.

The *ngamu* is considered the more dangerous of the two masked devils. It is known as the Zo *noi sheng* because it is controlled directly by the Poro hierarchy. The devil wears a warrior's costume of leopard skin sewn onto red leather, with side eye blinders and a flat, round cap. The gown is placed over a red cloth, signifying that the *ngamu* is itself a Zo, for only they are permitted to wear that color during Poro *meni*. The *ngamu*'s legs and feet are raffia covered, and its arms are hidden, showing only cow-tail whips. The mask has a moveable jaw with teeth. The latter are considered to be the objects by which the boys received their markings. The jaw of the mask is covered with raffia to resemble a beard. The nose is long and pointed, and the eyes are surrounded by white rings resembling the clay that is often used as medicine covering. As this devil performs, the mask is always in front of its face and is never moved.

The *Ngwalapiye* can be seen by members only, except for one ritual a year, when he lays a special sacrificial vine called *pala* around the community. The *pala* is laid along the same route each year, and bypasses the new parts of the community. After laying the vine, the *Ngwalapiye* puts a bunch of palm nuts tied to a bridge above each of the major paths leading to the community. Should anyone have an evil intention toward the town, he allegedly will be caught by the sacrifice and die. The medicine works to catch those who "have ever eaten palm nuts or tasted palm oil." This, of course, is the primary oil used in this part of West Africa, so it is taken for granted that the protection works on everyone.

There is another ritual in which this devil makes an appearance. This is just before the initiates into the Poro are reborn and given new names at the conclusion of the year-long rituals. Nevertheless, during all other performances of the *Ngwalapiye*, women and nonmembers are strictly forbidden to see it perform and must remain indoors until the ritual is completed. Often when there are "closed doors," the devil performer does not wear a mask. Instead, he walks about the town making the sounds of *Ngwalapiye* and thereby creating an auditory illusion. Those sounds are a loud, continuous trill that is then translated by the *kwelebah* to the community at large. The *ngamu*'s language follows the five-tone pattern and syntactic structure of normal Kpelle talk. The use of tone and other paralinguistic cues in the trill language often makes the talk understandable without the *kwelebah*'s official translation.

A definitional problem about what constitutes a separate society arises in regard to two other devils, the *Kaaipulu6alang* and the *Malangawlaw*. Both are considered to be the "wives" of *Ngwalapiye* and are often simply referred to as *ngamunea*, or *ngamu*'s wife. The *Malangawlaw*, an unmasked devil, is known as the wife who sings for her husband when he enters into town and walks through the community at night. The sounds that *Malangawlaw* makes are horns blown in unison by a small group of musicians who accompany the *Ngwalapiye* performer. Although the sounds are of four distinct musical instruments, all informant descriptions refer to the auditory effect as being a single devil.

The other wife of the *ngamu*, a masked devil called *Kaaipulu6alang* ('seeing behind devil'), is the so-called dancing devil that performs during all major celebrations, visits from prominent people either from the government or other communities, and funerals of Zo and other important elders. Membership in the Dancing-devil Society is restricted to men, but women and noninitiates are permitted to witness the devil's performance (in contrast to the other wife and to the husband, *Ngwalapiye*).

The *Kaaipulu6alang*, like the *Ngwalapiye*, has its feet and legs covered in raffia and wears a warrior's gown, but it does not wear the red cloth. Rather, it has a black gown, which is worn underneath the warrior's clothes. Its arms are extended and also covered in raffia. The mask is either worn on top of the performer's head or placed in front of the face, depending on what the devil is doing in the ritual. The dance is mostly a continuous spin. As the devil runs, the *kwelebah* and his assistant beat it with cow-tail whips; in this phase, the mask is placed on top of the head. The performer's face is covered with a black cloth with two small, white openings for the eyes. While the devil walks about the area or kneels before the musicians, the mask is placed directly in front of the face. This devil has a long cow-tail bush on top of its head, which flows partially down its back.

The rituals surrounding the two *ngamunea* can be considered to comprise two internally separate societies within the larger Ngamu society inasmuch as the members do recognize themselves as a distinct unit and inasmuch as rituals must be performed before membership in the units is recognized. On the other hand they contrast with the major *lalaa* society, the *6alasilangamu*, in that members join the latter group independently of the *Ngwalapiye* society and have their own Zo leadership. Even though all the major Zo of the larger Ngamu society belong to the *6alasilangamu* association, they are reordered according to a different structure of status positions and speaking prerogatives when that society's *meni* is the grounds for the social gathering.

The fifth devil is the possession of the third separate *lalaa* society, which is called the *Baiyaemu*. This society is only active during the Poro society initiations every generation. The society has a separate Zo who is not a member of the Poro Zo patrilineage. In Sucromu, the person who holds this office is the son of a deceased Zo that was, however, from a different lineage and quarter than the other Poro Zo. Membership in this society is inexpensive compared to the costs of joining the other societies. The boys who are initiates in the age-set community for the Ngamu society are able to join this society for an even lower fee. This devil is considered to be able to fly about the community to capture initiates who are reluctant about joining the Poro or who are from families who cannot afford the financial costs of having their sons join. The *Baiyaemu* is not a masked devil, for it can only be seen by its society's membership. When it makes an appearance in the town, the crier announces that nonmembers must enter into their dwellings. An auditory illusion is produced that corresponds to the nonmembers' account of the devil as one who flies from one part of the community to the other. This is done by the membership dividing into two groups and stationing themselves on opposite sides of the town. The members of one group blow a horn and chant in unison, creating the image of a large and powerful figure. Then, at its second blow of the horn, the group ceases its activity and immediately becomes still. The second group then blows the horn and begins chanting.

The Sande is the women's counterpart of the Poro. All women are required to join. In contrast to the Gola and Vai Sande associations, there are no masks associated with the Kpelle Sande. Initiation involves taking the novice into an age-set community in the forest near the town, where they remain for up to a year. There, they undergo scarification along the waist and a clitoridectomy and are later reborn back into the community with new names. Traditionally, the Sande bush lasted for three years. Since the period of modernization, however, the Sande bush, like the four-year Poro bush, has been reduced to one year only. Although many of my informants maintain that this reduction was the result of government intervention, several people in the government who have direct responsibilities for the Poro and Sande deny that the one-year rule was ever formally established. Instead, the reduction appears to be the consequence of a decision by the communities themselves in response to modernity. During the last Poro initiations, the now-deposed President Tolbert strongly encouraged a return to the longer bush period. Several in government hoped to use the extended time as a device for teaching literacy and other modern skills. One difficulty with such a proposal is the great cost borne by the families of the initiates and the time that youth would have to spend away from helping their families with the farming.

While the Sande bush is in session, the women are officially responsible for the moral well-being of the community. Anyone who commits a crime against a sacred ruling structure is first brought before the women; then, if the offender is male, he is tried by the Poro Zo. A portion of any fines levied must be given to the women. Although there is no devil directly associated with the Sande, a society called the Mina does have specific duties to perform for the women while their initiation bush is in session.

The so-called secrets of the Sande are analogous to the secrets of the Poro. Both societies provide their members with instructions in how to practice secrecy and assume their respective gender roles. The most active part of the Sande society is actually a *lalaa* association, the *Zohii*, that can be considered the women's equivalent of the *ɓalasilangamu*. It is composed of all the important Sande Zo and other powerful and important women in the community. Membership is matrilineally determined, as are the female Zo positions within the Sande itself. The Zohii has the responsibility of maintaining and guarding the women's fence, which is in the center of the town, next to the ricebird tree. This fence surrounds a small thatch hut which, in spite of its size, is reputed to be able to hold the entire female population of the town of one time. There is only one male who is permitted inside Sande activities. He is called *ɓelehaai* and is equivalent to the woman member of the Poro, the *tipinenu*. The *ɓelehaai* acts as a liaison between the Sande and Poro leadership. In the same way as the *tipinenu* is ritually referred to as a male, he is always called by a woman's name, and he acts the role of the nonsexual husband of the women Zo.

Related and Subsidiary Societies

Outside of the Poro and the Sande are the six *fe lalaa ni* societies. Membership in them is strictly voluntary, and their Zo recruitment is based on interest rather than any kin-based order of succession. Some of these societies have specific duties to perform for the Poro and Sande by protecting their respective bush schools and the community at large from malevolent spirits and other invaders from the outside. In addition, they have specific functions to perform for their own membership, and these functions are outside the influence of the Poro. Each of these societies can be considered independent of the Poro and is ruled by its own leadership. If two such organizations should enter into any conflict or palaver, however, it is the Poro leadership that adjudicates the matter and renders the final judgment.

The first two of these societies are related to one another in that membership in one is a prerequisite for joining the other. Prior membership in the Poro is absolutely required for initiation. These associations—the Moling, or Spirit Society, and the Mina, or Horn Society—also function, respectively, as the old and young men's warrior societies. To join the Moling, a man must first be a member of the Mina. Women may also belong to the Moling; they must first belong to the Sande and its internal Zohii society.

The Mina has the responsibility of warding off a particular kind of metaphysical danger, *wulu nuu* ('stick people,' or "witches"). The Kpelle maintain that each human has both a dream and waking spirit, or *lii*. For some people, the dream *lii* is known as *polo sheng* ('behind thing,' or animal dream spirit). These people share some of the physical or personality characteristics of their *polo sheng* and allegedly are able at night to appear as animals. The Kpelle often account for illnesses and death among these people by blaming a hunter for killing or wounding their dream *lii* in the night. Other people have human dream *lii*, and certain of these belong to a special dream secret society of fellow *wulu nuu*. Members are required to present a human sacrifice of some member of their patrilineage's dream *lii* to that society in return for wealth and power. The Mina society protects the town from such people, but individuals must seek protection privately from the blacksmith, who is one of the main Poro Zo and also a Zo of the Mina society.

In the Mina initiation, all members run through the town behind a *wulu nuu* devil. Unlike the other masked and nonmasked devils discussed above, this devil is not referred to as a *noi sheng*. When it comes out, the society crier announces that all nonmembers must go indoors just as for the Poro devils. There is a similarity between this manifestation and the *Baiyeamu* in that there is an intentional production of auditory illusion. As the members run through the community, they follow the Zo, who blows on a specially designed horn that produces a high-pitched sound resembling a terrified humanlike scream. The members, as they run, slap their arms against their sides, which produces a beating noise. The illusion produced is that of the members beating the *wulu nuu* (also referred to as *wiki*).

The primary responsibility of the Moling society is to keep watch over the major secrets of the community. Because both the important men and women of the community are members of the Moling, most serious discussions of a highly discreet nature requiring the presence of both sexes are held within its *meni* organization framework. It is also in this society that the belief in spirits is recognized differently from other community members. While many may believe in the actual ability of spirits to appear in the community, the members of the Moling are actually the ones who produce ancestral manifestations as illusions similar to the various devil manifestations. In a sense, Moling members are the most existentially aware cohort of the entire community. They produce spirit manifestations to accomplish community ends.

It would be an error to assume that these societies exist to trick nonmembers. When an initiate joins the Moling, his or her belief in the ancestral spirits does not diminish even though he or she now understands that the presence of such spirits in the community is the result of manifestations produced by the society. Welmers (1949) describes the society as organized to "fool the women" and make them believe in the powers of the men.[7] Although this is perhaps one of the functions of their evening ritual, the society also has the major responsibility for protecting the community and the Sande bush from invasion. In addition, the young men who are members are allowed into the outer fence of the Sande bush school to carry in supplies and other needed objects. The society is mainly active when the Sande bush is in session and only rarely meets during other occasions.

The Moling society is something like a council of elders and important personages of the community. The cost of initiation is very high. The society has the supernatural responsibility of protecting the town from malevolent ancestral spirits reputed to return to the community to exact some vengeance. Like the Mina, the society only protects the community as a whole; individual protection must be obtained privately from a Zo. Thus, if someone claims to have seen a deceased relative's spirit in a dream (or in a hallucination while awake), he is treated separately from the society. Sometimes when a member of the community violates an ancestral law, members of this society attempt to scare the violator by coming by his windows late in the night and pretending to be the ancestral spirits coming to seek revenge. Such violations include trespassing into the sacred sections of either Sucro or Twasa mountain. Only Zo and selected elders are permitted access to some areas in those locations. Also, should someone possess an object belonging to a deceased person, the Moling society might take action.

The other four societies have both a curing and a metaphysical function for the community. The most active at this time in Sucromu is the Kawli Sale, or Iron Society. This association also goes by the name Gbo Gbling. The Zo operates a special oracle, known as the *faa sale*, that possesses certain members. The Zo or the *bakung* (second or assistant to the Zo) speaks directly to the oracle to discover the metaphysical reason for some petitioner's troubles. The oracle is able to tell whether a person's illness or problems are the result of either *jina* or water people. There is a large typology for kinds of *jina* and two varieties of water people: *mammy wata* ('mammy water,' or mermaid spirit) or *nyai nenu* (water woman), and *kakelee*. Whereas the former enters into a dream sexual relationship with men, the *kakelee* affects both men and women by promising them in their dreams that in exchange for the spirit of a relative they will be rewarded in their waking lives. Once the supernatural agent responsible for a person's trouble is discovered, the Zo of the society is able to prepare curative and protective medicines. The society also has the responsibility for protecting the community from such malefic spirits. Hence, it has a peripheral function to perform for both the Poro and the Sande bush schools when they are in their respective sessions. Both men and women are members of this society, but it is only men who become possessed by the *faa sale* and act as the oracles.

Another society is the Gbo Sale, or Lightning Society. This association offers protective medicines to members and has a large corpus of poisons and antidotes. Power is symbolically expressed in the major public ritual (seldom practiced in the past few years) wherein all members put a bowl of rice in the center of the town and invite everyone from the community to put poison inside of the food. The members then collectively eat the meal without any harm. The society, as the name implies, also has medicines that can control lightning. Members claim to be able both to protect the town from lightning and to direct lightning to strike an enemy. This society has only male members.

The Snake Society, or Kale Sale, in Sucromu is recognized to be of Mano origin and outside, albeit under the indirect authority of, the Poro. From comparison with Harley's (1941a) description of the Bakono, the Snake Society among the Mano, it appears that many of the Kpelle Poro functions that parallel the Bakono are held by the Kpelle Iron Society, or Kawli Sale.[8] In Sucromu, the Kale Sale is considered an important "medicine" society that protects people from snakebites, cures people of a spirit snake or *jina*, and can also cause snakes to bite people at the will of the Zo leadership. The Kawli Sale considers the Kale Sale's snake to be the female version of their own male powers. Both societies have effective medicine to cure bites and ward off snakes from farms, dwellings, and paths. The Kale Sale has both male and female members. Up until 1971 it represented an important political grouping in the community. Its most active members were the various groups within Yamii *koli*, and it functioned as a mechanism for the four subquarters within the quarter to hold internal and discreet conversations while being protected under the secrecy proscription of the association.

When the Zo of the Sucromu Kale Sale became ill, the association became less active. At the same time, one of the elders from upper Yamii, Kaboku, announced his more active Zo-ship in the Kawli Sale, whose main Zo was Torkalong, who resided in the Twasamu moiety. With Kaboku as the second Zo of the Kawli Sale, the Yamii elders (and on occasion other members from the other quarters of Sucronsu *taa*) were able to use that society and its *meni* as a substitute mechanism for such internal discussions.

The Gbling Gbe is a mock association for young boys. They participate before joining the Poro. Although there are no medicines that belong to the society, they do practice chicken sacrifices. The boys grab chickens that are wandering about the town, take them into the bush, kill them in a sacrificial manner, and eat them. If caught, they are not punished provided they can establish that their activities were part of the Gbling Gbe. The boys choose one of their number to act as the Zo and another as the *bakung*, or assistant. After their sacrificial meal they go about the town in a processional, copying the behavior of their fathers in the regular societies. In this manner, the boys learn what it is like to belong to the major societies and get their first experience with having to practice a version of the secrecy proscription.

There are several additional societies organized in less formal ways. They are mostly hunting societies whose Zo are reputed for their special abilities in the forest. They have medicines for a successful hunt, protections against getting lost, ways of warding off *jina* and other malefic spirits while hunting in the night, and various first-aid preparations for cuts, dysentaries, and the like. Because most successful hunters base their powers on medicines (*sale*), they are willing to share their "secrets" with others who are willing to pay to join their ad hoc society. Such payments usually involve a chicken, rice, oil, cane juice (rum), and a small amount of cash.

Kpaiyea and Its Secret Societies

Kpaiyea is a town about the same size as Sucromu, some forty-five minutes' walk away. For a number of years it was the home of the clan chief and the district commissioner. The town is situated on a hill that was traditionally surrounded by a fence to protect against invasion. Today, a portion of that fence still remains. The community is only about thirty minutes' walk from the Guinea border and, like Sucromu, has many kinship relationships with a clan on the other side.

The town also has both a secular and a sacred ruling structure, but there are significant differences between it and Sucromu. Like Sucromu, the town is composed of five quarters. Three of these quarters have the same names as those found in Sucromu, and the inhabitants of the correspondingly named quarters recognize each other to be of the same family. One of these quarters is Zoman *koli*, which also is the patrilineage for the Kpaiyea Poro Zo. Both Sucromu and Kpaiyea have several of the same societies, but there are no *6alasilangamu* and *ngamunea* dancing-devil societies practiced in Kpaiyea. Whenever there is a need for such devils to appear, the Sucromu Zo are petitioned and come, upon Kpaiyea's request and payment. Hence, Kpaiyea has only one masked devil, *ngamu*. It does have the other nonmasked *noi sheng: ngamu*'s wife the *Malangawlaw*, who sings for her husband, and the *Baiyaemu*. The town does have a Mina society that produces a spirit manifestation through the management of auditory illusion in the same way as the Sucromu Mina society.

Kpaiyea also has its own Moling, Gbo Gbling or Kawli Sale, and Gbo Sale. It does not have a Kale Sale. The Gbo Sale is especially important to the community and is more active there than in Sucromu's sister society. This is allegedly because of an incident that occurred in the early 1950s when a large cotton tree fell on their market, killing several people. The tree fell after being struck by a lightning bolt. Kpaiyea, being situated on top of a large hill, is much more subject to such events than Sucromu. The Zo of the Gbo Sale take an active part in making medicines to ward off lightning during the frequent lightning storms in rainy seasons.

Kpaiyea is distinct from Sucromu and the other Kpelle towns both in the same clan and in the same chiefdom because of the existence of a second Poro organization that parallels the Ngamu Poro society whose Zo reside in Zoman *koli*. This society is known as the Mandingo Poro society and maintains its separate membership and Zo leadership. All of its members come from one patrilocal compound, Maning *koli*. Although Maning is translated as "Mandingo," the residents of this quarter are not Moslem and do not identify with the other Islamic Mandingo residents of Kpaiyea. Rather, they consider themselves to be Kpelle and identify as such whenever they are outside the context of the community.

This quarter is one of the richest in the clan and was the home of previous clan and paramount chiefs, district commissioners, school superintendents, and educational elite in the modern sector. Historically, they claim to have come from Guinea, probably around the turn of the century, allegedly at the request of the townspeople. When they came, they integrated themselves into the town life and became known in the community as *loi kalong* and as the quarter from which the town chiefs are recruited. The family elders from this quarter, including the town chief, double as the Zo of their Poro association. Most of the medicine protections and community sacrifices are, however, handled by the Zoman Zo or the *ngamu* in its only public appearance in the community. During all other rituals, women and nonmembers are forbidden from witnessing the *ngamu* and its performance in the town. The only other exception to this is a ritual performed at the end of the Poro initiations, when the *ngamu* publicly appears in the community to announce that its wife is in labor and is about to deliver.

The members of Maning *koli*'s Poro society are never initiated into the other Poro society. Their initiation occurs one or two years after the Zoman Poro society is finished, just before the bush is turned over to the women for them to conduct their initiations into the Sande society. Their initiation ritual is also significantly different from that of the regular Poro society. The novices only spend one week in the bush school. Every morning they go into the bush for instruction and then return to the community at night. They keep away from the women of the community during this period.

Both Kpaiyea Poro associations require that their members be circumcised and undergo scarification. The Zoman Poro initiates are scarred in a pattern similar to those in Sucromu: on the back, neck, and chest. On the other hand, the Maning Poro initiates only undergo minimal scarification surrounding their genitalia and on their necks. Once one is a member of the Maning society, he is able to attend all functions of the other Poro society as if he were a regular member of it. Likewise, the leadership of the Maning association takes an active part in the high-level discussions and adjudications handled by the Zo of the other society. Members of the Zoman Poro are not, however, permitted to attend the special gatherings of the Maning society. This control over the Kpaiyea Zoman society is also recognized by the Sucromu Poro Zo. Members of the Maning are permitted to join the *ɓalasilangamu* and participate in the membership activities of the Sucromu Poro when they are visiting that community, but they are often restricted from participating in the high-level discussions and palavers. This is probably more because they are not citizens of Sucromu than because they are members of the Maning Poro.

The Maning society does not have a devil or *noi sheng*. When there is a need for "devil business," the *ngamu* of the Zoman Zo is called upon to perform. Hence, the Maning society has political rather than ritual authority over the other Poro association. Consequently, Kpaiyea has a tripartite ruling structure rather than the dual secular and sacred ruling structure of most other Poro communities. In Kpaiyea, the secular leadership of the community exercises political control over the sacred through the addition of the Maning society. This is in contrast to Sucromu and other neighboring communities, where the town chief's power is much restricted compared to the Poro. For example, the Sucromu town chief lacks power to require any cooperative labor. He may request his townspeople to help bring sand for a new clinic, brush the bush on the road between two towns, and the like; but any cooperation he receives is based solely on his charismatic authority and ability to recruit. On the other hand, if *ngamu* should make an announcement requiring community organized labor, all members will obey or be forced to pay a large fine by the Zo leadership. In Kpaiyea the chief and others in the secular ruling structure can, as members of the Maning Poro society, force cooperation by requesting the Zoman Poro association to make their requests for them. When that occurs, the Kpaiyea *ngamu* makes the announcement, and all men in the community are required to obey.

Besides the major differences in the organization and function of the Poro societies in Sucromu and Kpaiyea, there are also significant differences in their ritual behaviors. These differences are marked not only between these two communities but across the other towns in the clan. For example, only Sucromu and Salayea (the paramount-chief headquarters) have the *ngamunea* Dancing-devil Society. Likewise, only Sucromu has the powerful *ɓalasilangamu* society. Whenever other towns in the clan wish to have those *noi sheng* come to their communities, they must formally request it from the Sucromu Zo leadership. There are thus many ritual interactions between communities even though each Poro association is independent of the others.

Variations among Poro Societies

In this chapter, I have described how Poro members recognize a range of similarities and differences in the society as practiced in diverse communities and language groups. The Fala, who are one of five dialects of Kpelle speakers in Liberia, consider that the Poro among the Loma is closer to their own than that of the Mano. Concomitantly, they recognize the Mano Poro to be more similar than the Gola, and the latter to be closer than either the Bassa or Vai.

This raises questions not only about the common organizational features in the Poro but about the definition of ethnic and language groups. In Liberia, as throughout the west Atlantic forest belt culture area, there are no traditional political entities such as tribes. Instead, ethnic groups are identified by the languages they speak. Establishing boundaries of language communities is problematic, however, because it depends on whether one considers that a particular community speaks a dialect of a given language or a different language altogether. The only centralized political structures that exist to unify communities are those imposed by the federal government. Clans and paramount chiefdoms were organized by the government according to the languages spoken in an area, but the larger political divisions of district and county cut across them. These artificial political divisions resulted in a wide range of cultural differences existing between speakers of the same language, while many recognized similarities obtained between neighboring groups speaking different languages.

Although there are organizational similarities in most communities where the Poro is practiced, these do not provide criteria for actually defining Poro. If, for example, common practices such as the existence of the lengthy bush school as part of the initiation process, the existence of different types of bush-things or devils, a differentiation between sacred and secular leaders (i.e., Zo and chiefs), scarification of the necks and backs of all new members, and dual sacred organization of the Poro and the Sande were taken as the definitive features, then the Maning society in Kpaiyea could not be considered part of the Poro.

Poro members throughout the Loma area do recognize the Maning Poro's legitimacy even over the societies of other language groups that manifest all or some of the features above. Thus, a Maning Poro member can participate in discussions and rituals of any Poro group in each of the towns in the general area, whereas a Bassa or Vai Poro member may be excluded from them. This points to the importance of geographical proximity as a crucial variable in how members decide whether a particular Poro society is relevant to their own. Earlier, I mentioned that there is a close relationship between the Poro in Sucromu and the Poro society in the Loma town of Malawu. The two associations share many of the same medicines and, for certain high-level discussions, meet as coparticipants in the same group under a commonly recognized leadership. Thus, Poro can cut across language groups if they are near enough to one another.

Although a list of common structural features can be given for the Poro, these do not constitute what a Poro member necessarily takes into consideration when he decides whether someone from a different language or ethnic group is a legitimate Poro member. This raises the methodological issue of whether to accept the structural similarities as criteria for defining Poro or to rely on members' judgments alone. The latter do not fully characterize the organizational distinctions between Poro and Porolike associations, yet ignoring them will produce a definition of Poro that can only be typological.

I thus take the view that any single structural description of the Poro is inappropriate and incomplete. Instead, the Poro should be considered a diversity of associations that differentially share some ritual practices. These associations differ from other societies in that they have the capacity to establish communicative and political alliances with each other that transcend ethnic and linguistic boundaries. This capacity is based on geographical proximity coupled with recognition of shared ritual practices and the mutal constraint to practice *ifa mo*, or secrecy, regarding each other's activities.

4
The Concept of Secrecy in Secret Societies

A major concern when writing about secret societies is how to avoid being accused of unnecessarily exposing secrets. It is crucial, therefore, to understand precisely what members mean when they refer to their secrets. This is especially important for the Kpelle of Liberia, who practice some ten-to-fourteen secret societies at the local level. Although secrecy is relevant to virtually every aspect of daily life, the Kpelle have no single word for secret. Instead, they use the phrase *ifa mo*, literally translated as 'you cannot talk it,' as their warning to practice secrecy. It is employed not only in discussions about secret-society and medicine matters, but as advice for using discretion when discussing mundane social relationships and events. When an initiate joins a secret society, he is given a medicine potion, called *kpEla*, which he drinks over a display of medicine objects, or *kafu*. On this occasion *ifa mo* is formalized as a rule. The initiate first swears that he will not describe anything seen inside the society fence or house. He then promises to tell the other members of the society any information he learns that could be used against them. Finally, he swears to tell of any impending danger to the community.

When an initiate joins, he thus swears both to talk and not to talk. Choosing to speak is a reflexive feature of the settings in which he finds himself, for on those occasions he is asked to say something if only to demonstrate that he is a legitimate member. Every member must decide whether he or she has the right to talk during each interaction. Information that on one occasion is a "do-not-talk-it" can, in another situation, even with the same participants and in the same physical setting, be acceptable for discussion.

Each potential speaker makes the decision of whether to talk or not largely by identifying the particular auspices of, or meaning context for, the social situation. In Kpelle these auspices are called *meni*, which I translate following Schutz's (1962, 1967) use of the concept "multiple orders of social reality."[1] We all participate in a variety of such orders, ranging from the world of everyday life, fantasy, and dream, to that of science. Each order is, as Gurwitsch (1964) describes it, an "intrinsically connected and coherent realm or domain exhibiting unity and continuity that is describable according to one's experiences of context and of indefinite continuation of context" (p. 401).[2] Goffman refers to these domains as frames (1974).[3] The Kpelle recognize a large number of different social realities, whose contents can be so expressed. Each of the varying orders of reality, or *meni*, provides a different meaning context, both for producing and for interpreting the meaning of talk and the symbols used in ritual activity.

There are basically two classes of *meni*. First, there are those whose identifications are instances of a speaker's formulation about the purpose for an interaction. For instance, if two hunters are discussing a kill, they might label their discussion as *sua paa meni* ('meat-killing' *meni*). Here *meni* is similar to one of Goffman's frames. The topic provides a meaning context that can be encompassed within a variety of larger frames. Where Goffman speaks of embedded frames, Gurwitsch makes a distinction between "thematic fields" within "orders of reality." Several different thematic fields can coexist within the same reality, and the same field may exist in different types of orders of reality. In the above example, *sua paa meni* can be part of any one of a number of larger *meni* that encompass it. Killing animals can be part of a sacrifice, the activities of a hunting secret society, the instruction of a father to his son, and more. The use of *meni* as a conversational formulation is a thematic field in this sense.

The second class of *meni* is a set of formally recognized types of interactional circumstances. A litany of formal *meni* types is obtainable by attending to the responses to a question-salutation that is asked whenever a Kpelle speaker meets another, either for the first time in the day or after an extended absence, when walking into a medicine fence of a secret society, or when entering someone's house. The question asked is *Ku meni naa?* (literally, 'What is the *meni* there?'). Usually, the response is *Meni nyomo fe zo* ('There is no bad *meni* inside'). If, however, the participants desire to exclude the questioner from the setting, they will answer by giving one of a number of *meni* names. These might include the names of any of the secret societies. For instance, if a nonmember should happen upon a gathering of the Lightning Society, the members will respond to his question-salutation with *Gbo Sale meni kaa ti* ("That is Lightning Society *meni*"). Likewise, if someone should happen upon a serious family discussion, he or she will be informed *Kala meni kaa ti* ("That is family *meni*"). After receiving such a reply, the questioner normally will excuse himself and leave the setting. The naming of *meni* on such occasions thus operates as an exclusion device.

When a prospective participant is informed that "there is no bad *meni* inside," it is, nevertheless, crucial that he determine which *meni* serves as the grounds for the interaction. Should he make an incorrect assessment, he might be accused of exposing secrets, abusing others in the setting, or challenging them to a status contest. The inappropriate taking of a speaking turn can be interpreted as an abuse or as a call for a test of power between the speaker and others who claim to have greater authority within the setting's organizational *meni*. This is similar to Albert's (1972) description of Burundi rhetorical processes in which turn-taking order is determined strictly by a person's "seniority."[4] In the Kpelle case, "seniority" is determined not only by relative age but by which *meni* serves as the grounds for the occasion. Depending on the *meni*, the order of speaking prerogatives may shift even among the same participants. Thus, under one *meni* a person may be able to discuss a certain topic and render judgment but, under another, be restricted from speaking about the same topic.

I have recorded a palaver that exemplifies the effect of *meni* on the right to talk (Bellman, 1975). The matter was adjudicated in the Poro court between the Snake Society Zo and one of the members. The Snake Society had finished a meeting and were dancing in a procession through the community. The Zo gave the order that no one could take any food, only drink cane juice. When the group greeted the town chief, he offered some food, and one of the members insisted on his right to eat. The Zo accused him of a serious abuse and sued him in the Poro society court. The member argued that, because they were outside of the Snake Society medicine house, the organizational *meni* was *taa meni* ('town' *meni*) not *Kale Sale meni* ('Snake Society' *meni*). The defendant did not deny that he had disobeyed the Zo. His sole defense was that, under *taa meni*, the Snake Zo had no right to restrict him in his activities. The Poro Zo eventually judged in favor of the Snake Zo. In so doing, he recognized that it was indeed *Kale Sale meni* that was the organizational basis for the procession.

Often the very formulation of a *meni* is a method for determining both the jurisdiction and the outcome of a court case or palaver. In a different case, I recorded two elders in a dispute about medicine ownership. One of the men, Mulbah, visited his friend, Kokulah, and spent the night at his house. The next morning Mulbah left town to visit relatives in a distant Loma community. That night, when Kokulah went to bed, he found a medicine object lying on the floor and placed it near his own medicines.

The following week, Mulbah returned, but Kokulah said nothing about what he had found. A short time later Kokulah became ill and sued Mulbah in the town chief's court for leaving a bad medicine in his house. Mulbah argued that if Kokulah would give him back his medicine the illness would cease. Kokulah refused, saying that he did not have to return the medicine and that Mulbah should be held legally responsible for his suffering.

After both men gave their respective testimonies, the chief decided the matter should be heard in the Poro fence. This change of jurisdiction shifted the *meni* grounding from town to Poro. Whereas under the former, Mulbah had a right to recover his property, under Poro *meni*, he was responsible for the problems his medicine caused. By determining where the dispute was to be heard, the chief implicitly rendered his judgment. His choice not only established the status and seniority order of the setting but provided an interpretive framework for deciding on the rules of evidence relevant to the case.

In each of these examples, the discovery of appropriate *meni* was critical for determining the intended meaning of the talk in the respective settings. Likewise, what is considered to be "do-not-talk-it" is grounded in the *meni* that provides the organizational basis for a given interaction. Every *meni* is recognized by members as transcending local situations. Members are able to change *meni* informally by acknowledging that a certain topic's appearance in an interaction requires the recognition of a specific society *meni*. They can also change *meni* through the implementation of "secret" signs. The latter instances include those in which members of a society decide to initiate their association's *meni* as a method of insuring that what they are discussing is under the protection of the *ifa mo* proscription for their group.

Instructions for establishing the presence of a particular societal *meni* are given as part of the initiation oath ritual. New initiates swear "to talk" any information that could possibly endanger a fellow member. Members introduce such warnings by proffering any one of several signs learned during the initiation instruction. These signs might include such acts as turning a particular piece of furniture in a certain direction, pointing to a section of a specific leaf, displaying a special hand gesture, or changing some part of a handshake. Because every society has its own particular corpus of signs, the ability to use them and to recognize their presence are methods of displaying membership. When members of a society want to make their discussion confidential, they need only produce one of these signs, and their shared societal *meni* will then serve as the new organizational basis for the social interaction. The establishment of that *meni* as the meaning context leads to an immediate restructuring of the order of speaking prerogatives and rights to talk in the setting.

The Evasive Secret and the Search for the Corpus

Simmel (1950) differentiated secret societies whose presence is known but whose membership is confidential from those in which the membership is known but the activities are secret. Examples of the former include illegal political parties and various other outlawed groups. Although the Poro is an instance of the latter, illegal secret societies do exist in Liberia. There are various reports of associations that practice such acts as human sacrifice for the preparation of medicines. The government has campaigned to stop these groups and has recently prosecuted several of their practitioners. Although the government treats the illegal societies differently, they share many features with the legal secret societies: internal social organizations as well as members' beliefs about how medicines (*sale*) and sacrifices (*sala*) work through a power (*kai*) that is in the control of their respective Zo leaders.[5] The legal societies do recognize the potency of the illegal medicines made from human parts. They, too, have medicines to advance the prestige of members and to guarantee their success in attaining jobs, love, and luck; but rather than prepare those medicines from human parts, they use animal sacrifices. Thus, the distinction between the two types of associations is not qualitative. In fact, many of the legal societies, including the Poro, openly practiced human sacrifice in the past (Harley, 1941b). Today, the legal societies recognize the authority of the government and the laws against performing these rituals. Simmel's distinction, therefore, is based more on a society's legal acceptability than on any actual structural difference.

In the course of my years of research in the Poro center of Sucromu, I had the opportunity to join several secret societies. Initially, I accepted Simmel's characterization of the novice as one who only slowly gains access to what is really secret in secret societies. In several of the groups I advanced in the hierarchy, and in two I apprenticed myself under their Zo in order to gain access to the knowledge they possessed. Over time, I gained expertise in the use and preparation of the various societal medicines. Initially, I thought that such medicines were the "real" secrets, which only experienced members had a right to know. I learned, instead, that any member with knowledge of the medicines can reveal to nonmembers almost any of the numerous curative, protective, and offensive medicines. The only requirement when showing a medicine to a nonmember is to collect some payment and not to mention that the preparation is part of the society's repertoire of medicines.

After a time, several people in the community sought my advice for their medical problems. This was in contrast to my previous experiences, which I shared with most other expatriate ethnographers, of being almost continually asked for first-aid knowledge of Western medicines. Instead,

I was being approached as a knowledgeable member of the secret societies. Despite this recognition, I anticipated that I eventually would be told secrets beyond those I learned during my initiation. Finally, I realized that my knowledge of the secret societies had become more extensive than that of many of the other members.

The secrets I was told when initiated into the societies were different from what I learned during my years of affiliation. The former were primarily methods of displaying membership. One of the most protected items of information in any Kpelle secret society is the description of a medicine object called *ngung sale* ("head of the medicine"). This is a fetish object that contains a portion of each of the numerous leaves used to prepare the society's repertoire of medicines. The ability to select the *ngung sale* from among a group of similar-looking medicine objects is both a display and a test of membership. Should a member of another community decide, during a visit, that he wants to participate in the host community's organization, he first will be tested to find out if he is, indeed, a legitimate member. The test includes his correct selection of the society's *ngung sale*.

After a new member joins a society, additional information will be given if he is willing to pay for it. If a member desires to become a Zo, he must learn all of the society's rituals and the preparation of each of the medicines. To acquire this knowledge either he will pay a Zo to teach him, or as is more common, he will serve the Zo in exchange for the apprenticeship. The knowledge gained by this process is distinct from the secrets used to display membership. Although the various leaves and preparations learned are not necessarily concealed information, what is *ifa mo* is that they belong to a corpus of medicines possessed by the society and constitute, in part, its *ngung sale*. Thus, a nonmember may unwittingly learn several of a society's medicines by paying money or by trading medicine knowledge of his own.

The Ability to Know

Though a person may purchase or be shown a medicine, this does not necessarily mean it will work for him. In virtually all of my interviews and conversations with societal Zo, I was told that each person has an inherited ability or right to know certain medicines and not others. This ability is called *kasheng*. It is because of this *kasheng* that medicines cannot be stolen. When one decides to teach a medicine to another, it is considered necessary that he first speak to the leaves to inform them that the learner has a right to know and to have them work for him. The manner in which the leaves are approached is crucial, according to members' belief systems, to whether the medicine will work for the person being taught the preparation. Often, the same leaves are used by different secret societies for a variety of medicine preparations. When teaching the preparation of a medicine, the instructor must approach the leaves in the manner determined by membership in the appropriate society, normally by first giving the society chant. The chant is used for all societal functions and must be sung before a member can speak. Thus, a member of the Kawli Sale chants *zinc ka zinc, kanbe ka kanbe*; a member of the Kale Sale, *gboga hey mensia, gboga hey mensia, heit may kasia gbo*; a member of the Gbo Sale, *gbing gbili gbee gbee*; or any of several other chants for each of the different associations. If the wrong chant is given, the medicine allegedly will not work even though prepared using the correct formula.

When the instructor is going to teach someone a medicine preparation, he first tells the leaves the amount of money he is to receive for his work. The student is not present during this conference. After being shown the leaves, the student is told to talk to the leaves before picking them. Instead of giving a societal chant, the student names the person who instructed him and states the amount he paid for the knowledge. In this way, the medicine becomes anonymous, and its possession by a particular society remains unrevealed to all but members.

There are certain medicines, among these, the Poro and Sande medicines, that work only for people from particular families and lineages. Only the Zo of the Poro are able to make their societal medicines work for the benefit of the community. To be a Poro Zo one must come from the Zo patrilineage and must usually be the eldest son of a member of the Zo hierarchy. Although a Zo usually chooses one of his own children to take his place, his selection is made on the basis of the child's interest and ability to work with medicines. The Sande, or women's, medicines are transmitted in a similar manner except that the line is passed from mother to daughter instead of from father to son. Such medicines thus work as a result both of the inherited prerogative to know and the intellectual ability and motivation to learn. Should a non-Zo witness a Poro and Sande Zo prepare his or her medicines and then attempt to copy the process, the medicines allegedly will not work. Medicines, therefore, cannot be called secret in any strict sense, as their preparation is not actively concealed.

What is secret depends heavily on the *meni* that serves as the meaning context and organizational grounds for a social interaction. Therefore, what members of a secret society will consider to be *ifa mo* is problematic. A person's speaking prerogative, right to talk, speaking-turn order, and the manner in which he or she approaches a topic all are determined by the *meni* that is recognized. For some people, any discussion about society matters to an outsider is to be avoided, whereas other people are willing to discuss issues openly without any thought that the *ifa mo* proscription is in any way violated. Often, the Zo of a secret society is more willing to talk, on the basis of his highest speaking right. In contesting a Zo's decision to talk, an accuser would have to assert a speaking prerogative above that of the Zo. The determination whether a piece of information is secret is, therefore, an intentional decision made within each interaction. This is evident in the following description by one of my Kpelle field assistants of how the Poro can work to conceal knowledge:

> Say if there were an automobile accident on the road and some townspeople were killed, the news would first be carried to the town chief. He would call the big Zo of the Poro and they would close doors in the same way as if the devil [ngamu] was out of its fence. When all the women are inside of their houses, the Zo tell the close friends of the family of the people who were killed. Then, they call the wives and mothers of each of those killed and take them to a place where the friends are waiting to tell them what happened. That way the friends are there to help them with their grief. If the Zo did not do this, the women would probably kill themselves.

The Poro provides a mechanism for controlling the flow of information. The devices used for that purpose are more important than the information that is concealed. Any item of information is a candidate for being a secret; it is the way in which the information is concealed and discreetly communicated that marks it as such. Thus, secrecy is best understood according to the methods used to withhold and convey knowledge.

The Transmission of Secrets

When I first joined the secret societies, I often tried to anticipate the rules of secrecy to be followed. I discovered that even some knowledge I thought to be confidential was discussed outside the medicine house in the presence of nonmembers without any claim that a breech of the *ifa mo* proscription was made. It was then that I became aware that *ifa mo* pertained not so much to concealing content as to intentional structuring of communication. One of my initial experiences in how to practice *ifa mo* was when I took the oath of membership and was informed about the *ngung sale*. Because it is normally *ifa mo* to describe the object discursively, the Zo instead provides the initiate with instructions in how to locate it. In so doing, he communicates not only which object is the head but the social organization of the society. The following is excerpted from my field notes when I joined the Iron Society, or Kawli Sale.

After entering into the society house, I was told first to kneel before a display of medicines. Torkalong, the Zo; Mulbah, his assistant or *bakung*; Folpah; and Labulah were all present. Tor-kalong told me to pick up the *ngung sale*. I looked over the some thirty-odd objects laid out neatly on a mat before me. I reached for one. Suddenly Mulbah shouted at me that the medicine be-longed to him and to leave it alone. Then, I reached for another. This time Kokulah loudly rebuked me, saying that I had pointed to his medicine. Again I selected, but this time Folpah claimed that I had chosen his medicine. I pointed to another, and Labu-lah scolded that it was his. Finally, I pointed to a medicine that was not as impressive looking as the others. When I proceeded to pick it up, Torkalong quietly said that this was the head.

Through that process I learned what was *ifa mo* without anyone having to verbalize formally what was not to be spoken. It was always crucial for members to be certain whether they have the right to talk as well as the right to know. The two are not necessarily related. Nonmembers very often know some of the secrets of membership; yet they must maintain a description of the event comparable to that of naïve nonmembers. This was expressed directly to me by one Kpelle assistant in his discussion of the women's knowledge of the Poro initiations. During their period of seclusion in the bush, the boys are, according to the women, dead, to be reborn the following year in an elaborate rebirth ritual where they receive new names and responsibilities. My informant discussed the women's knowledge of the seclusion as follows:

Many of the women know that the boys are in the bush. They are only told that they are killed by the devil [*ngamu*] and will be reborn later. But the women are not stupid. They see us carry rice and oil to the forest every day. They must know that the boys are there. It is just that they cannot talk it. If they do they will be seen as exposing things.

Thus, the women may know the secret and have a member's interpreta-tion of the situation. Both realities coexist: the boys are metaphorically dead, and the boys are in the bush. The ability to formulate the secret and the public right to know which definition is relevant are a direct conse-quence and display of membership.

The use of indirect forms of communication to convey concealed information extends beyond the formal rituals of the secret societies into the discourse processes current in everyday life. For instance, inasmuch as the Kpelle are polygamous, there tends to be a high rate of marital infidelity by secondary wives (Bledsoe, 1980; Gibbs, 1962, 1963a, 1963b, 1965). When a man discovers that his wife has a lover, he can demand an adultery fine of ten dollars from her paramour. If, after the fine is payed, she continues with the affair, the husband can demand a return of bride-price and a much larger fine. Very often, however, a man is aware from the start who his wives' lovers are; for sometimes a woman will request that a prospective paramour be willing to have his name confessed to her husband before she is willing to have sexual intercourse. After the lover makes the payment, the husband knows, but does not talk, about the lover. He can, as a result, request that the lover assist him on his farm and with other chores. Should the lover refuse or mistreat the wife, his name will be confessed a second time, and he will thus suffer a severe fine or have to do enforced labor for the husband. Consequently, the information that one's wife has a lover becomes a "do-not-talk-it" that is indirectly discussed both with the wife and the paramour. Many of the same message forms that appear in the societal rituals are applicable to this kind of situation.

In the following chapter, I examine a large variety of adumbrated message forms along with the procedures that members use to locate their intended and situational meanings. Although my final focus is on the transmission of information about and during the Poro initiations, the various practices I analyze are relevant to other occasions where secrets are communicated. Together they constitute a corpus of procedures for disclosing concealed information without exposing it. For this reason, I refer to these practices as the language of secrecy.

5
Secrets as Texts: The Message Forms of Deep Talk

Secrets usually are communicated in indirect ways. They are transmitted either through verbal statements or ritual performances that allude to the concealed information. In this chapter, I demonstrate how secrets can be treated as texts by describing the different message forms that are used to communicate in an indirect or adumbrated manner. These message forms are used both in naturally occurring interactions and in informant descriptions about concealed cultural practices.

Very often, people treat informant descriptions as if invariant to context and transcendent to the occasion where they are produced, but any formulation is always doing something besides that about which it tells.[1] Ignoring the intentional structuring of informant accounts results in narratives about particular events becoming generalized into normative principles. For example, Harley (1941a) describes in a general rulelike fashion what happens to a woman who accidentally discovers what occurs inside the Poro initiation bush and refuses to practice the do-not-talk-it:

> She was caught and tied. Her relatives were notified and asked to bring a quantity of salt, four loads of rice, pepper, palm oil, beni seed, and a cow. Then the woman was killed anyhow, and was eaten in a great feast in the Poro. If the woman's people were wealthy or influential, they would possibly save the woman's life by paying three more cows, but the woman could never speak again as long as she lived. She was given some kind of "medicine" which paralyzed the organs of speech, or more scientifically speaking, she was probably hypnotized. At any rate, she never talked even one word to anyone. If she did she would have been killed and she knew it. She could not even talk in her sleep! (p. 14)

This narrative appears to be more an account of a particular occurrence that graphically describes a punishment for talking than a general rule about what happens in situations where women discover Poro secrets and speak them. Although Harley states that this is a secondhand description of what traditionally occurred in the Mano Poro, he does not provide the context in which the story was obtained. Instead, he presents it along with other descriptions of the social organization of the Mano Poro and the meanings of the masks without ever differentiating between the kinds of elicitation occasions where each type of information was obtained.

In the Poro culture area, accounts very often are told to emphasize particular points even though the speaker did not actually experience the narrated event. I have recorded numerous narrations ranging from accounts of the past, when Zo were reputed to have possessed supernatural powers now lost, to present-generation exaggerated descriptions about contemporaries. Such talk is normally not interpreted in the same manner as more straightforward narratives. Instead, it is the idea or theme of the account that is considered significant. These narratives adumbrate meaning and are part of what, in Liberian English, is called "deep talk" and, in Kpelle, is *Kpelle wo su ɓela* ('split Kpelle words').[2] Understanding them involves the same interpretive procedures as does the discovery of intended meanings in parables, proverbs, chants, ritual metaphors, and dilemma tales.[3] These procedures are the primary methods of communicating concealed knowledge without being accused of exposing secrets.

I am not claiming that Harley's description of what happened to the woman is necessarily invalid or untrue. It is possible that it is a straightforward narrative about Mano-speaking peoples' practices instead of an adumbrated account. Without knowledge of how the story was obtained, however, we can only speculate as to what Harley's informant was intending in presenting him with that story. I have also obtained an account of a woman's death as the result of having violated the *ifa mo* proscription. Analyzing it demonstrates how such accounts are intentionally structured to communicate more than a direct interpretation of the talk would yield.

Three Versions of Kapu's Death

Kapu was a young mother of approximately twenty years of age. She lived in the patrilocal compound adjacent to the path where the new initiates were led from the village into the initiation fence. She had been living with her husband, a soldier, in Monrovia and decided to return to her home at the request of her mother to assist in preparing her young brothers for the initiation. The families of the initiates are required to provide rice, palm oil, and different kinds of meat, poultry, and fish throughout the period when their boys are in the bush seclusion. Kapu returned home in time to help her mother and sister plant and harvest the year's rice crop.

Kapu was very excited when it was time for the first of her brothers to join. When the Poro officials came and ritually captured him, she tried to stay as close as possible to the town celebration and playing. After he went into the bush, she remained in town for the rest of the day. The following morning she started to hemorrhage. When the bleeding became severe, her father called in a medicine Zo. Later that afternoon several Poro Zo came to her house. Then, in the evening, she died.

I first learned of the death when I was visiting with the town chief. A young man from Kapu's quarter came to inform the chief about what happened. He announced that she had died from hemorrhaging. Everyone commented on how terrible it was that such a young mother had died. Later in the afternoon a close friend of mine from the deceased woman's quarter gave me an account of how she had died. He said that she was caught by Zo's medicine because she had too closely followed her brother as he left town and went behind the Poro initiation fence. I asked if he was suggesting that the Zo had purposely killed her. He answered that she died for being too close to the Poro medicines.

Later, in the early evening, I and some other friends from the community paid our respects to the family. After we left their house, a man from Kapu's quarter who accompanied me provided a different version of the death. He said that Kapu died because she had witnessed Poro secrets in her dream. I asked what she had seen, and he said that she had seen her brother enter behind the initiation fence and enter into the bush-school community where the other initiates were sequestered. When she awoke she told no one of the dream. Then, a little later, she began to hemorrhage. When a medicine Zo was called, she confessed over his oracle that she had seen her brother join in the dream. It was then that several of the Poro Zo were called into the case. By the time they had arrived and begun to prepare their medicine cures, it was too late.

The next day, Kapu was buried. At her funeral no mention was made about the unusual circumstances that led to her death. A few days later I was at the town chief's house with several other men when the topic of the death came up. All expressed how sorry they were about the death and were quite concerned about the child. I asked what they thought the cause of her illness was, hoping that I would be able to clarify the two stories I had obtained. Instead, I received a third, more secular, account that did not address any Poro-related issue. The person who answered stated only the official facts of the case: that "Kapu died from hemorrhaging after only a day's illness." He admitted that it was an unusual death, particularly for such a young woman. When I asked if he did not think that she was killed by medicines, he agreed to the possibility but did not bring up the knowledge that her death was somehow related to the Poro. From that time, I never heard anyone mention any Poro issue as a factor in the death.

I refer to the third account as "secular" because it does not involve any mention of cause underlying Kapu's illness. It is not really opposed to either of the other two accounts; after the funeral, the interpretation of cause simply was no longer relevant. The incident was treated similarly to descriptions of court cases or palavers after adjudication. Both litigants during the course of a palaver are usually quite vocal about their respective positions. After a case is decided, however, the official version as established by the chief or other adjudicator is what is used in all further accounts of the case. Only when a case is appealed to a higher court is a matter still open to divergent interpretations. When a matter is considered closed, only the formal facts of the case are relevant to any account given about it. In a like manner, after Kapu was buried, the matter was for all practical purposes settled. It was no longer relevant whether Kapu died because she physically was present when her young brother entered into the initiation bush or because she was there in her dream. No one can accuse a Zo of killing someone except, under special circumstances, another Zo. Because many considered the death to be part of Poro *meni*, it no longer was open for discussion after the Poro Zo was finished with the matter. Thus, only the fact that she had hemorrhaged to death after a single day's illness was significant to any account of what occurred.

The two accounts of cause given before the funeral were different but not necessarily contradictory. The Kpelle, like many other groups in the culture area, treat their dreams as having a facticity analogous to everyday reality.[4] As I explained in Chapter 3, everyone is reputed to have two "brains," or spirits: one for dreams and one for the world of daily life. People are alleged to be able, in their dreams, to affect changes in the waking world. Those who, in their dreams, do evil actions that cause harm to others are called *wulu nuu* ('stick people') or, in Liberian English, "witches." To say that Kapu had followed her brother into the initiation fence in her dream would be as real a statement as to say that she was physically present when he entered. Thus, the second account could be a version of the first or easily have evolved from it.

I was present and video-recorded the initiates being taken from the community, and I walked past the house where Kapu was living. I did not witness her following the boys from the town, nor was I aware that she was anywhere near them as they entered behind the initiation fence. When I heard the first account, I thought perhaps that I did not happen to see everyone in the area. Most of the women who were either related to the initiates or friends of their families were together at the other end of the quarter, where they chanted and danced until the *kwelebah* came back to town with his announcement that the boys had successfully entered into the bush. Some of the women, however, stayed near their houses as the boys were paraded through the town. These rituals are discussed in the following chapter.

Both accounts of Kapu's death are consistent in telling what can happen if a women gets too close to the boys. No woman is permitted to interact with the initiates once the *kwelebah* puts a thatch sash, or *japa*, around their necks. The unusual circumstances of the death were accepted by many townspeople with either interpretation. Coming too close to the initiates in a dream has the same consequences as coming into direct physical proximity. As it was doubtful that Kapu actually followed her brother into the forest, the second version of the death appears valid. To accept that account necessitates a recognition of the dream world of reality whereby Kapu's hemorrhage and subsequent death could result from her dream brain having come into contact with the initiates. Because she did not immediately upon waking confess what occurred, she was caught by the Poro medicine and bled to death.

Another possibility is that her confessions were structured by the divination process. According to the second account, Kapu confessed to having had her dream before the oracle of a medicine Zo (*sale* Zo). Although I was not physically present, I did learn about what happened from a member of the extended family, the person who first presented me with the second version. I had previously attended numerous sessions where clients and patients of different Zo had consulted with their respective oracles. These sessions included several consultations with the spirit-possession medicine, the *faa sale*, in the Iron Society and numerous sacrifices before *mina sale*, or horn medicines, for protection against different spirits and other forces, or *kai*, in Kpelle cosmology.

In each instance where an oracle was consulted, the interpretation was first presented by the oracle worker and then accepted by the client. Most interpretations involve the client admitting to having had contact with a spirit in the dreamworld. The following is one instance I personally witnessed and recorded in my field notes. Torkalong, the Zo of the Iron Society, asked me to participate in a *faa sale* oracle consultation. As a member of the society I had a right to be present, although normally only those who have a special interest in the case or are assistants to the Zo attend. I had been apprenticed under Torkalong for several months at that time to learn the necessary corpus of leaves that constitutes the society's *ngung sale*. I had attended several consultations before this occurrence and have attended many since, but this one dramatically exemplifies how the consultation is done.

When I arrived, Torkalong had taken off his shirt and was sitting on the floor in front of Flumo. Flumo had complained that he was suffering from lack of energy and wasn't able to work well on his farm. Tokpah was sitting next to the Zo. Suddenly he began to enter into the trance state. He became very stiff and began to pound on the sides of his head. Then, Torkalong took the *faa sale* medicine and placed it into his hand. The medicine had a bell attached to the end. Tokpah shook the medicine, ringing the bell next to his right ear. In a high-pitched falsetto voice, he gave the society chant and began to speak as the spirit of the medicine. He said that Flumo had a relationship with a *nyai nenu* or mammy water. This is a spirit that enters into sexual relationships with men in their dreams and can cause them great harm or trouble if they become angry with their dream lovers. Tokpah said that Flumo's *nyai nenu* had given him a cowrie shell for good luck. He found the shell by the waterside after having received instructions in a dream. Flumo agreed that this was true. Then, Tokpah jumped up, went into the next room, climbed a ladder, took down a suitcase, and produced a cowrie shell. Flumo admitted that this was the shell he found after his mammy-water dream lover told him where to look for it.

Sometimes a patient will confess before a second oracle if he determines that the first Zo's medicines are not effective. In another instance that I recorded, a man named Flumo died even after having consulted two different oracles. In the first consultation, he confessed over a *mina sale* that he was a *wulu nuu* and had in his dream killed his newborn infant. When he failed to recover from his illness, he consulted a second oracle belonging to a *teli pe nuu*, or sand cutter type of diviner.[5] In that divination, he was told that the reason the child dies in the dream is because his wife had a relationship with a different kind of water spirit—a *kakelee*. This spirit is reputed to offer wealth and prestige to those with whom in dreams it contracts to receive the human soul of one of their relatives. The patient also accepted this interpretation at the time of presentation. After he died, everyone I interviewed about the case claimed that both oracles were correct—the wife did have an arrangement with a *kakelee*, and Flumo had killed and eaten the infant in his dream.

In both the *faa sale* possession and the *mina sale* sacrifices, the clients confessed only after the interpretation of cause was given by the oracle operator. Likewise, Kapu confessed over an oracle that provided her the interpretation that she was ill as the result of having come too close to the Poro medicines during the initiation of her brother. Her acceptance of the interpretation was an acceptance of the Zo's medicines. The confession was a necessary prerequisite before the Zo could begin his cure. Although her condition continued to get worse, her family did not consult a second oracle. The medicine Zo's diagnosis was not at issue because her illness was divined to be the result of Poro medicines. Because the Poro has control over all other medicine matters and secret societies, every *meni* is subservient to it. When the medicine Zo decided that Kapu was not responding to his cure, he called on the Poro Zo for assistance. In so doing, he did not change the interpretation of the cause of her illness; instead, he admitted that the Poro, as the superordinate *meni*, had to participate directly in the cure. Kapu's willingness to accept the Poro Zo's help was a continuation of her acceptance of the oracle's interpretation. Likewise, the Poro Zo's willingness to intervene without consulting a separate oracle demonstrated their concurrence with the first oracle. Kapu's subsequent death was not blamed on their inability to help in such matters nor on the inappropriateness of the oracle's diagnosis. Rather, the Poro Zo claimed that before they could begin their respective cures under Poro *meni*, Kapu had died.

The three accounts of this case are each intentionally constructed narratives containing metacommunicative meanings that cannot be located by a direct examination of the respective texts. It would be inappropriate to accept any version to the exclusion of the others. The first account was contradicted by many community members, including myself, having witnessed her brother's entry along with the others in his initiation group into the bush. The second account necessitates a willingness to believe either that Kapu actually followed her brother into the initiation fence in the dreamworld or that she had accepted an oracle's interpretation of what could possibly have occurred without her waking brain or spirit having to be necessarily responsible for her dream brain's acts. It does not account for the community's interest in the confession and why it was such a pervasive topic of public conversation.[6]

The official, or legalistic, account of the death does not contradict the other versions. Instead, it lends support to both by glossing over cause and admitting that the death was unusual. To argue that this case history is generalizable into a normative rule about what happens when women accidentally come too close to Poro initiation activity requires a selection between the alternate versions. If each account is instead treated as a adumbration that points to the possibilities of the kinds of consequences that can come from such close proximity, then each version is acceptable without excluding the others. The choice of one version over another is not based on the case history itself but on the ethnographic particulars within the interactional context wherein the account is presented.

The discovery of inconsistencies in narrative descriptions is a procedure for discovering that a speaker is using "deep talk."[7] That assessment is distinct from situations in which a speaker is thought to have lied. Lying is a serious abuse and normally is taken to court as a tort for adjudication. The distinction between statements that adumbrate and those that deceive involves different evaluative procedures. A lie, according to Bok (1979), is "an intentionally deceptive message which is stated" (p. 14).[8] Lying, then, is considered a subcategory of deception. Because truth or truthfulness is always relative, the principle of veracity cannot be used to distinguish lies from other statements that are constructively tailored to fit the exigencies of the situation. To lie is an intentionally distinct act. Likewise, any accusation that someone has lied denotes that the challenger has a different and competing account of some reality the accused also shares. It is incumbent on the challenger to demonstrate that the accused has intentionally presented a lie.

As a result, in Kpelle communities, such accusations normally end up in court. In most cases, the challenger is the defendant in the case; the accused sues the challenger for abuse and slander. Because most court actions concern cases where the accusation that someone had lied was made in public, there are always a sufficient number of witnesses willing to testify on behalf of the plaintiff. The act of abuse, rather than the accusation that was first made, is the tort that is adjudicated. The motivation of the defendant for having made the accusation and his evidence are tangential to the case and, depending on the rules of evidence established by the matter under dispute and their organizational *meni*, may not be fully presented in the palaver nor change the outcome in favor of the defendant.

The Hermeneutics of Deep Talk

When listening to "deep talk," hearers must attend to it as an analogical description that refers to meanings other than those contained in the narrative itself. I recorded a narrative that demonstrates how such talk is interpreted (Bellman, 1979). I summarize it here in order to introduce the kind of interpretive methodology that is used to pick out the intended meanings of such narratives. The incident concerned Torkalong, the blind Zo of the Iron Society. One afternoon he told several members of the society (including myself) how he first became the Zo of their association. He began by telling us that before his birth his mother had borne only female babies. She felt that it was necessary to have a male child to insure that someone would care for her in her old age. She decided to have sexual intercourse with her husband's brother; in that way, no legal charge of adultery could be brought against her lover. Just before her delivery in the resulting pregnancy, her husband tried to kill her. He was stopped by the townspeople, and Torkalong was born. Later, when Torkalong was about to be weaned, the husband tried to kill him but failed. Torkalong was blinded in the incident. When he was about grown, he dreamed that God spoke to him, saying that everything would turn out all right. The following day, the Iron Society performed in the community. The spirit-possession oracle, or *faa sale*, spoke directly to Torkalong. The society leaders were amazed, as they claimed that the medicine could only speak to the Zo or his assistant (the *bakung*). They decided that Torkalong must join the society and become a Zo.

The major inconsistency in Torkalong's narrative was that everyone present was well aware that he had in fact an older brother. In a subsequent interview with his brother I was told that the latter had become an Iron Society Zo before Torkalong. According to his brother, Torkalong had been blind since birth. Because he wanted Torkalong to be able to earn a livelihood, he taught him how to be a Zo in the society. This contradictory information disturbed no one except myself when Torkalong related his account.

Immediately after giving his history, Torkalong told a dilemma tale. Such stories are fictitious narratives that end in some dilemma the teller's audience must solve (c.f. Bascom, 1975). In this case, Torkalong told of an orphan boy that was the victim of a trickster opossum. The opossum stole a basket, or *kinja*, of kola nuts from a powerful chief and led a trail of the nuts to where the boy was sleeping in the forest. He placed a piece of kola in each of the boy's hands. The chief, upon discovering that a *kinja* was missing, sent his soldiers out to find the culprit. They brought the boy back to town and were about to execute him when an old woman asked that he first be permitted to mind her unbeaten rice. When the last of the rice was beaten, she gave the boy a portion to eat. Then, a cat came and asked the boy to give him the rice in return for saving him. The boy gave the rice away and in return was given a dead rat. Then, a snake came and made the same offer. When the boy gave it the rat, the snake said that the following morning it would bite the chief's favorite wife and then gave the boy the medicine to cure her. The next day the woman was bitten and died. When she was about to be buried, the boy brought her back to life with the medicine the snake had given to him. The chief was so happy he rewarded the boy with half the town. Then Torkalong asked, "Who was the main person responsible for the boy being a man today—the old woman, the cat, or the snake?"

The answer to the dilemma tale, when applied to Torkalong's first account of how he became a Zo, turns the latter into an analogical description rather than a straightforward history. The answer that all finally agreed upon was that it was the old woman because she was the first to offer the boy aid. Her structural position was as the originator of the action. This in turn defined the organizational *meni*, which can be inferred as *nuu poloi meni* ("old-person" *meni*), that was the meaning context for the boy being saved. Her seniority established the *meni* structure. This procedure of locating "person responsible" or originator of action to locate a specific *meni* is also used to discover which *meni* is the basis for a given social interaction, particularly when the *meni* is not named in response to the *Ku meni naa?* question-salutation mentioned earlier. The location of the originator of action provides an interpretive key to understanding Torkalong's account of how he became a Zo. In comparing the dilemma tale to Torkalong's narrative, his mother's husband's actions were in the same position as the opossum's acts to the orphan. Concomitantly, God's intervention and assurance to Torkalong in his dream was structurally equivalent to the old woman's intervention for the boy. In this manner, Torkalong intended that God was both responsible for and the source of his Zo powers. Hence, he claimed that his powers were based on God, or *Xala meni*, rather than on Iron Society *meni*.

This claim is particularly significant in light of the typology of types of Kpelle Zo. First are the inherent leaders of the Poro and Sande societies. Second are those who join a society and eventually purchase its *ngung sale*, which normally requires that the owner not only gain an expertise with the society's corpus of medicines but possess many of his own that do not belong to the society. Third are those persons who possess medicine knowledge that is not associated with any of the secret societies. This knowledge is considered *kasheng* and cannot be transmitted except to one's children (men to their sons, women to their daughters). Those who possess an unusual amount of such knowledge are called "Zo for God" (*Xala* Zo). Very often *Xala* Zo join secret societies and purchase the head of their medicines in order to use the associations as personal medical practices. Any member of the medicine societies can purchase the *ngung sale* and thereby become a Zo. To establish a practice independent of other Zo, it is considered necessary, however, to first possess knowledge of medicines other than those belonging to the society's corpus. Thus, many of the *Xala* Zo establish their reputations by becoming secret-society or *sale* Zo. This was Torkalong's claim in his analogical story and dilemma tale. Whereas the Iron Society protects the community from various malefic nonancestral spirits, Torkalong also has his own cures, which are independent of the society, for numerous mundane illnesses including amebiosis, snakebite, convulsions, and fevers as well as medicines for warding off malefic spirits and protections against poisons and other types of "bad medicine."

Torkalong's dilemma tale, with its subsequently derived solution, provided his hearers with an interpretive key with which to locate the intended meaning of how he became a Zo. That key transformed his narrative into an analogical account. The historical verifiability of the facts in the history gave way to the interpreted sense of the narrative. Because all present were aware of the counterevidence when Torkalong presented his history, they implicitly understood his narrative as an instance of deep Kpelle.

The dilemma tale Torkalong told has several answers. The solution is accomplished by the participants in the situation where the tale is presented. Depending on the particular meanings the teller is intending, other solutions are possible. The opossum and orphan story was not of Torkalong's invention. Bascom (1975) pointed out that a version was collected as early as the turn of the century on the Kru coast. Members use such tales strategically within social situations. Inasmuch as the answers are negotiated within the interactional setting, hearers attend to the background structure of the telling situation for the solution rather than to the propositional structure of the tale itself.

The Location of *Meni* as Meaning Context

Thus dilemma tales can serve as one of several available devices for establishing which *meni* is the relevant meaning context for interpreting the intended meaning of an adumbrated account. In many accounts, interpretive keys are located within a text rather than, as in the above example, in a separately told narrative. The following excerpt of a letter sent to a Liberian student from Sucromu living in the United States exemplifies how instructions for interpretation can be embedded in a text. The student's mother's brother's son, whom the student referred to as his *ngala*, or "uncle," wrote the letter. The writer lives in Monrovia and works at the Ministry of Information as a news editor. He receives enough of a salary to rent a room with electricity that serves as a meeting place for many of the other labor migrants from Sucromu who come to Monrovia to work and attend school. Because of the ongoing flow of people from Sucromu with whom he is in contact, he always has updated information about the community. The following is the letter he wrote to my assistant, whom he calls Andray, in which he uses deep message forms to communicate the most important items of news from home:

Dear Andray,

To continue the news from Sucromu, let me begin with this: I bought the five bundles of zinc that I promised for the building of the house I promised. Sam just wrote telling me how some friend are helping him collect materials.

I left Jerry in Sucromu. He is there to spend sometimes. I wanted to know how he and Louise were coming and he tells me that she is still his wife.

*His other girl, Buju's sister is now one of Flomo Morowolo's
wives.*

*My son, Papee is now talking but not to well he calls both me
and his mother Deddeh.*

*I want to let Nuta come and attend school here next year
because as I see it if he stays up there he will be totally useless to us
and himself.*

*If all work well, I want to go back to school next year because
my interest in becoming a business tycoon is great. Therefore I
want to hold a degree in it.*

*Pekin's grandfather Koomorwor Gbamakena died on the 25th
of October. This is again another time of festivity for the zoes of
Vavala Clan. As you know he was the oldest of them all in the
whole clan. There is also another one died in Teleman but I do
not know his name.*

*James M. Folpah's little sister Suah got missing some part of
last week for about two days and was at last found in the Tor-
hamu Forest sitting on a log one afternoon crying. This is how she
got missed, they (she and some other children) were playing in
the moonlight**think on ABC on Liberia the book we took in the
2nd grade 'it is the new rice that get the villagers to dance to the
beat of the drum in the moonlight' that is it is now harvest time in
Sucromu**when the same dwarfs that are always killing the
children in their quarter took her away.*

*Mortor was here for the weekend of Oct. 25: he asked me to
send to you this letter of his.*

*Be good and be serious about your lessons. Translate this
parable in Kpelle and get for yourself the meaning: taking a knife
from its pack is a shameful business.*

Roland

The first part of the letter contains a relatively straightforward description of information about the writer's family, news of my assistant's
brother and his wife (Jerry and Louise), the writer's intention to bring
Nuta, my assistant's youngest brother, to Monrovia, and the writer's
intention to return to school. The news about Koomorwor Gbamakena
appears at first glance to be a direct descriptive obituary without any
hidden meanings. Read in the context of the background cultural information about Poro leaders, or Zo, however, the paragraph takes on
different meanings. The rural peoples of Liberia have only been keeping
records of births for the past generation, and so the concept of "oldest" is
relative according to one's seniority and position. Thus, Gbamakena's
being the "oldest" refers to his position in the hierarchy of Poro Zo.

Whenever a Zo dies, it normally is suspected that he was killed by another Zo. At Zo funerals it very often happens that a Zo from another community will confess that he was responsible, and because Zo are expected to have protective as well as offensive medicines, a Zo who kills another cannot be held legally responsible. Consequently, the cooccurrence of the report of the Teleman Zo death indicates that the deaths were the result of Zo warfare, in a similar manner to the warfare between the Malawu and Sucromu Zo discussed in Chapter 3.

Although the above requires readers to trust in the interpretation of my two assistants and myself, which was also verifed by subsequent visits to the field after the letter was written, the following paragraph about James M. Folpah's little sister Suah clearly demonstrates the use of indirect forms of expression to communicate a news event. The letter writer uses a parable within a narrative to describe a historical event. The first sentence locates the personage and event within the setting. It has a literal sense that contrasts with the other sentences in the paragraph. Each of the other sentences is metaphorical because its meaning cannot be located by a direct examination of the linguistic code. Rather, these sentences require the reader to employ an interpretive methodology that is reflexively provided for in the text. The first part, or the subject phrase, of the second sentence also has a literal value; yet it differs from the first sentence in that the writer compounds the sentence with a section that provides the interpretive instructions necessary to understand the predicate phrase. He does this by marking off those instructions with double asterisks.

The asterisked section is itself broken into three parts. The first establishes the meaning context for the second part. This turns the latter into an adumbrated parable description rather than a literal account of events that occurred. The second part serves to reformulate the first but carries information contained only in the second part by virtue of its being an adumbrated description. The three parts taken together establish the appropriate *meni* meaning context for deciphering the predicate phrase (which stands outside the second double asterisk). The second part of the section contains a hidden premise that presents the interpretive key with which to understand the predicate phrase. That is, during times of major celebration (such as harvests), special sacrifices (*sala*) are made to ancestors and spirits (*jina*) in gratitude for their assistance. The predicate phrase can then be interpreted as revealing that the child was sacrificed to *gbaima*, or dwarf spirits. The child's quarter is reputed to have quarter secret societies who base their powers on alliances to and reverence for such spirits.

When I asked the letter's recipient my purposefully naïve question— why the writer did not just state directly the news of the child's sacrifice—

he replied that "one does not just broadcast openly such things." An omnipresent feature of Kpelle talk is the recognition of the practice of *ifa mo*; the extensive use of metaphorical descriptions is, then, a member's method for accomplishing it. Such talk, or "deep Kpelle," is often a source of complaint for Kpelle speakers in the modern sector when they visit communities in the interior, for the use of such speech genres relies on members' recognition of the intentional structure of each interaction occasion.[9] That intentional structure includes not only the background knowledge about the history of previous interactions between speaker and hearer, but the hearer's personal biography, his previous relationship to the topic discussed, the particular *meni* meaning contexts where both speaker and hearer confronted the topic in the past, and the organizational *meni* that provides the grounding for the current social interaction.

The paragraph that gives advice to the reader about his studies in the United States also demonstrates the importance of *meni* as the intentional structure for social interaction and demonstrates still another interpretive methodology. The parable as translated into Kpelle reads: *e boi kula danga gaa e wungma meni*. Its transliteration is: 'you the-knife take-out-of the-pack it-is shame *meni*.'[10] The last two words of the parable, *wungma meni*, pose "shame business" as a kind of *meni* category. Rather than shameful (*wungma*) being an adjective for *meni*, it refers to a particular category of *meni* in the folk taxonomy of kinds of *meni*: namely, one that is structured by shame. In elicitation sessions with representative samples of elders from various quarters, there was unanimity that *wungma meni* was originally associated with acts of warfare.

Until the federal government of Liberia pacified the area in the first half of this century, wars were fought in a determined pattern. First, a warrior known as a *kukulah* was sent to walk the path between his town and the one to be attacked the next day. He would always carry a small sword (also called *boi*) as a symbol of his position. Whenever he came upon a farm owned by residents of the town to be attacked, he would stop to receive hospitality. If offered, he would warn the people that his town would be attacking their's the following day and that they should escape from the area or be killed. When the *kukulah* reached the town to be attacked, he would take his "knife from the pack" and announce the coming battle. The people then had the choice of abandoning their community or preparing for war. If they were to kill the *kukulah* or refuse to fight the next day, it would be considered *wungma*.

When a town attacked another, the first warriors into battle were called *kolibah*. These warriors dressed in special costumes with headdresses that prevented them from looking to the side. This same costume is worn by the *ngamu*, as he is considered to be a warrior for the Zo when he engages in the type of mock battles discussed earlier. Once these warriors "took their knives from their packs," they could not retreat, as to do so would be considered *wungma*. Thus, to take a knife from its pack is to commit oneself in such a way that all next acts are structured by the principle of shame. In Andray's letter, "taking a knife from its pack" is in a metaphorical relationship to "be good and get serious about your lessons." Both are member categories belonging to the same *meni* category.

Hard work is considered analogous to warfare. This is expressed in the dual use of the term *kuu* for the cooperative work societies organized for making rice farms and for a group of warriors formed to engage in *koi*, or warfare. Likewise, the Poro initiations are called *kuu*, as the initiates are taken from the community to engage in a battle with the *ngamu*. Because the receiver of the letter had come to the United States under my sponsorship to complete his education, his family considered that his success would benefit everyone, as most youth in his community are not fortunate enough to attend school, and of those who are able, less than 15 percent go past the sixth grade. Thus, Andray's work in school was considered analogous to the actions of the *kukulah* and *kolibah*, as they were the first warriors to engage in battle. Once Andray (or Yakpazuah, his Kpelle name) committed himself by coming to the United States, he had withdrawn his knife from the pack, and in so doing there is no retreat. To fail would be *wungma*, and thus his education was structured by *wungma meni*.

The applicable methodology for understanding the advise paragraph is opposed to the interpretive methods used in understanding Torkalong's adumbrated story and dilemma tale, where the metonymic relationships between themes in the story are directly analogous to the relationships between themes in the dilemma tale (i.e., the father's actions were analogous to the opossum's acts in causing harm to the respective *dramatis personnae*, as were God's actions to the old woman's intervention in the account of the dilemma tale by changing the situation from bad to good). Likewise, in the paragraph about James M. Folpah's little sister Suah, the instruction section provides a parable: "it is the new rice which gets the villagers to dance to the beat of the drum in the moonlight." The interpretive methodology described above shows how that phrase adumbrated a hidden premise: during times of celebration, special sacrifices are made to allied spirits and ancestors. Here, "new rice" is in a metaphorical relationship to time-of-celebration, as is "dance to the beat of the drum in the moonlight" to forms-of-celebration—which includes sacrifices. Likewise, the adumbrated section as a whole—location of meaning context that makes the second phrase a parable that in turn provides information for the reformulation that established the event time as harvest time in Sucromu—is in an analogical relationship to the predicate phrase of the second sentence.

Although there are different logical strategies employed to decipher the meaning of deep Kpelle codes, in each instance the correct location and formulation of *meni* serves as the interpretive key to understanding the talk. In locating the appropriate *meni* the auditor or receiver of the message draws from his or her own position within that order of social reality. Thus, one may be able to locate a *meni* but, because of nonmembership or having a low status within it, still not be able to decipher the message as intended. Deep talk, therefore, involves both an understanding of message forms used to convey the information and an assessment of the membership that the speaker and auditor make in regard to the *meni*, which serves as the interpretive key for understanding those messages.

Pretalk, or Preface Sequences to Formal Discourse

Besides having to locate organizational *meni* in narrative descriptions, it is also important to establish *meni* during formal discussions, rituals, palavers, and court actions. Earlier I discussed two examples of palavers where the choice of *meni* resulted in the respective outcomes for each case tried. One of the ways that participants in a formal discussion establish an organizational *meni* is by engaging in what my Kpelle research assistants called "pretalk," or preface sequences to formal discourse. Often, elaborate preface discussions negotiate in an adumbrated manner which *meni* is to provide the meaning context for the formal discussion, as in the following transcript segment of a video recording of a discussion held in the palaver house of Waiquai Vallai, who is the *loi kalong* for Sucromu and also the ex–clan chief of the Vavala clan.

VALLAI: I cannot forgive anyone. If I forgive someone, he will always feel that I am afraid of him. I cannot forgive anyone except for myself.

TOLPAH: That is the truth.

VALLAI: Now if you would have called someone to come, the person would say, "I made it possible for Vallai to agree what you begged for." I gave the gun to Kanangxali and Kanangxali used the gun. He never for one day brought me meat (takes off hat), until he became a dead man [died].

TOLPAH: He became a dead man.

VALLAI: Are you with me?

TOLPAH: Uh huh.

VALLAI: They didn't bring it to me.

TOLPAH: Yes.

VALLAI: I went to Kpaiyea about the gun *meni*, so they told me to sue Kanangxali. He killed meat until he died. Then you want me to sue, then it is the whole house business [*pele lee zu meni ka ti*].

TOLPAH: Uh huh.

VALLAI: I said, "No, I cannot sue." It remained like that until someone came and he said I thought they were going to kill me.

EVERYONE: (Laughter)

TOLPAH: I said, "No. Everyone can do wrong."

EVERYONE: Uh huh.

VALLAI: If you do anything, they cut your head [i.e., people will always be critical of an adjudicator]; what they do depends on what you say. If they say [threaten] to you, and you say a person cannot do anything to me, they will talk about what you said to them. God sent everyone his own way, in order to do something. A person cannot do what his friend does. If someone calls you for rice every day, you are supposed to call him [favors must be reciprocated]. Good *meni* only on you now [may you have good luck].

EVERYONE: Uh huh, uh huh.

VALLAI: Every time I talk to my *maling* and *longi* [children], that if they are working for me, I pray that the person can stay a long time. I say what it is, the *meni* I talk is some of it. "If," I said to them, "you are the workers now. I cannot be a worker anymore, unless these people, the *maling*, say they will work for me for a long time." If you serve me, God my body is good [I am healthy], you can wash me [i.e., give protection; "to wash" means with medicines in this context], these people now can wash me, God my body is good. In the morning I see food, then my body is good.

MULBAH: You are old now . . .

EVERYONE: Uh huh, uh huh, uh huh, hhah haa.

BAKOLEE: It washes all the clothes [all is well].

VALLAI: Do it. Hey, Kokulah, your younger brother is here and said it is not you who did it. He said your wife is here, this business what your wife is doing, and this business that is happening, is your wife doing it? What is she doing for me? Have you asked her, "Are you serving my father?"

BAKOLEE: Ee aah (laughter).

VALLAI: Then, she cannot pass you if she isn't serving. The rice you cooked, are you serving him?

KOKULAH: She serves him [*E gaw ke*].

VALLAI: She serves him.

BAKOLEE: Uh huh, eh, then, you are doing it.

VALLAI: No, no, no, no, no, hey, stop it here. If food is here, if it is like this that is given to him [one must deal with the way things are].

MUWULU: This is given to me take it there (turns away in opposite direction).

VALLAI: Uh huh, take it and carry it there.

MUWULU: Eee.

MULBAH: She cannot now be mean to him.

VALLAI: Do you think she'll be mean again? Then, you ask her.

EVERYONE: Mmm.

VALLAI: When night comes now, if that is small like this, she will say, "Here is some small; come carry it there" [a good wife will give what she has to offer]. It is good. It is the one a long time ago, we came and saw it outside [in the traditional way]. But it is not outside now [things are not as they traditionally were]. These times it is hard everywhere, and unless someone thinks about it, let us lay it where it was laying [not make an issue of it]. When you take it small, then you are on it the old way [by not making a minor dispute into a major court case, you are doing things in the traditional way]. (In a quiet voice) Let us think on it.

EVERYONE: Uh huh.

VALLAI: (In a whisper) The *meni* that is not there is not there; the one there, that is what we will do. We are hanging head [deliberating] on it.

KEPE [a female in the group]: I am saying something.

ONE DAY: We will go to hang head. Father Muwulu?

MUWULU: Mmmmm.

ONE DAY: (Handing some coins to Muwulu) It reaches you.

FLUMO: They are taking your picture.

MUWULU: Our voices are being recorded.

BAKOLEE: The way is there.

(Inaudible)

BAKOLEE: Let us think about it. The one there, let us talk it.

(Camera pans to Yakpazua; he and Muwulu are speaking to each other—voices inaudible.)

YAKPAZUA: It is what we are talking.

MUWULU: It is land business. If you reach it to me [ask me about it], I understand (Vallai temporarily leaves the room).

(While Vallai is out of room, general cross-conversation, camera turned off; then on to Muwulu talking.)

MUWULU: You, the land, people, it reaches everyone. If the matter is twisted, it is just the head [important matters are complex by nature].

YAKWOLO: It is it . . .

MUWULU: This is the place where I have come.

TOLPAH: Is the chief in the fence?

FLUMO: He is.

TOLPAH: Call him to come.

MUWULU: The matter did not start on this spot. It was a long time ago. It moves there. Vallai knew something about the *meni*. The reason I say he should come, that is the reason he should come. You hear it good? An argument is on it. There is a day to create a fight. The explanation . . .

KOKULAH: Someone is on it.

MUWULU: You there I can shame a person! If I am talking, I am not reaching it to you. If a person doesn't want it, he shouldn't call me to his palaver [if you don't want to listen to my opinion, don't call me to participate in your palaver]. A person talking, a person doing that to him [interrupting], it is a different matter. They can kill someone in it [for it].

TOLPAH: It is you *maling*.

MUWULU: No it isn't *maling*.

KOKULAH: It is I.

MUWULU: I hear you said to him your *ngala* Kokulah, he stands up and comes and disturbs; they think we don't know business. (Pause; he then begins his testimony:) I have land but at that time Dadamanang was the first man who fought for the land, and his sister who was One Day's wife. After he fought for the land, because she is a woman her name is not on the land. If she is driven from the land, it will go to me; if there is a divorce, the land will go together. One Day went to me and asked for the land. Since I gave One Day the land, since I was born has any-one heard of the land being divided between the sister and the brother. When my sister was small I fought for her also. *The buttocks are in one trousers but they are divided* [*Wulong gaa bele naa kawle*].The other side of the land is for the other people. All the kola trees on that land belong to me. They were planted by my father. The other people were permitted to use the land. I gave land to the Zoman people to let someone else work on the land. In case if I had some meat [animals] and it destroyed someone's property, who will they go to—won't that be me. Labulah was an old man; my name was put first on the paper. The first paper is not good now, so I went to Vanjaman [the county seat] to get new paper to show who owns the land. That is the paper I am using now to show who owns the land. The second paper, the teacher is fixing it.

TOLPAH: Which teacher?

MUWULU: Mulbah Sumo. Before they could copy it . . . it needed a typewriter. We went to James Flumo to get his typewriter. He sent us to Samuel Tablo to get a typewriter. After James typed the letter, he said we needed the clan chief to sign it. So we went to Vallai to sign it. When we went to Vallai to sign, Vallai said *wolo ho manang* [a geographical location belonging to Vallai's own patrilineage]. When Vallai said this, Labulah and I didn't say anything to him. That is what happened when we went to Vallai. All the witnesses concerning the land business did not swear on the medicine. Vallai charged them five dollars, five dollars each.

VALLAI: What business are you talking about?

MUWULU: That is just when the whole palaver was called.

SEVERAL PEOPLE TOGETHER: That is not what they even were in there for.

TOLPAH: No, he is trying to tell how his father got the land. They went to James Flumo, and Kwala asked if Nowai was the sister to Muwulu, and Muwulu agreed. Then Muwulu told Kwala, "The man who is working on the land, go sue him because he let someone work unknown to the one who was minding the land."

The discussion went on for some time, and a temporary agreement was finally reached establishing Muwulu's rights to certain portions of the land. When I returned to Sucromu six months later, the palaver was again discussed. At that time, the palaver was held before James Flumo, the new clan chief. It was decided that the land should be split according to the internal segmentary lineage structure of the patrilocal quarter.

It is my contention that the preface talk initially presented by Vallai is analogous to Torkalong's use of the dilemma tale as a device for establishing the appropriate context within which to locate the sense of his adumbrated account. When Vallai introduced the two topics of the discussion (the gun palaver and Kokulah's wife's disrespect for her husband's father), he established the *meni* meaning context and the rules of evidence to be used in the palaver to follow.

Vallai established that the gun palaver concerned *pele lee zu meni*, which is translated as the 'whole house business.' That is, it refers to a matter that has importance to the entire community rather than just to the litigants involved. In establishing the importance of the case he presented the legal grounds for suing in *meni* of that category. He presented the obligations that borrowers have when property is loaned, even if they are related to the loaner. Then he expressed how the lending of property benefits all parties when appropriate obligations are followed:

> Every time I talk to my *maling* and *longi*, that if they are working for me, I pray that they can stay a long time. I say what it is, the *meni* I talk is some of it. "If," I said to them, "you are the workers now. I cannot be a worker anymore, unless these people, the *maling*, say they will work for me for a long time." If you serve me, God my body is good, you can wash me, these people now can wash me, God my body is good. In the morning I see food, then my body is good.

By establishing that it is the responsibility of those who are under one's authority to care for their superior, Vallai expressed how the lending of property contains the same obligation. That is, when property is no longer used by the owner, it is the responsibility of those to whom it is lent to take care of the owner. This is the premise upon which items are lent in Kpelle culture. For example, the owner of a sugar cane mill always receives at least one-fourth of the distilled cane juice from those to whom he lends his mill. Likewise, if one gives a hunter shots for his gun, he will receive a large portion of whatever the hunter kills. Thus, although one lends property without any rental fee, it is always expected that the owner will receive a portion of whatever is produced.

When Vallai presented his gun-palaver account, he elicited agreement from all the setting's major participants including Bakolee, the corporate representative of Zoman quarter, the compound accused of misusing Muwulu's (Yamii) quarter's land. Vallai then turned his attention to the issue of recognizing the traditional interpretation of familial rights and obligations by asking Kokulah about his wife's alleged disrespect for his, Kokulah's, father. Again, after obtaining agreement from all the major parties, Vallai summarized:

> When night comes now, if that is small like this, she will say, "here is some small; come carry it there." It is good. It is the one a long time ago, we came and saw it outside. But it is not outside now. These times it is hard everywhere, and unless someone thinks about it, let us lay it where it was laying. When you take it small, then you are on it the old way.

He then introduced the matter to be discussed, and the palaver began between Muwulu, Mulbah, Kokulah, One Day, and Bakolee. In summation, it concerned a dispute resulting from One Day having permitted Kokulah, who was from Zoman quarter, to use land One Day was given for use by Muwulu's *kala*, or patrilineage. One Day's temporary rights to the land were upheld, but an apology was necessary for Muwulu because he was not asked about Kokulah's use of his farm. The case was more complicated than it appears at first glance, however. The palaver reflected a general disagreement about the lineage rights of certain portions of land originally part of the holdings of the larger corporation— the extended patrilineage. The case was adjudicated as a method of clarifying family rights and responsibilities during the then-forthcoming Poro initiations.

This case illustrates how palavers are often intentionally used as adumbrated accounts whose deeper meanings—the sense of the narratives— must be differently understood. The informal pretalk that prefaced the actual discussion about land tenure established the meaning context and rules of evidence relevant to the occasion. Later, these same interactants were involved in a discussion that resulted in a continuation of the dispute. After losing the case, Muwulu collectively sued each of them over a different, albeit related, issue. That matter involved Muwulu's suit against them as goat owners. For some fifteen years Sucromu forbade any goats from being raised in the town. Then, a now-ex district commissioner proclaimed that goats must be raised in each community to produce additional meat necessary for the Poro initiations then in preparation. Because the litigants in the above case were all rather successful farmers, they were the owners of most of the goats in that part of the community. Muwulu claimed that their goats had destroyed some of his property and sued them in Zorzor, the district headquarters. He won the suit, and so the litigants all went to Zorzor to appeal. While they were there, Bakolee left his associates and went to take care of some other business. When they came back to town, the others complained to Folpah the town chief.

In the same manner as in the matter adjudicated by Vallai, Folpah initiated pretalk that established both the *meni* and the rules of evidence relevant to the situation. Each of the participants told a story about his experiences with modern, or *kwii, meni*. Mulbah described how many years ago, they would blow a horn to announce *kwii meni* in the community. After discovering that most people would run into the bush to avoid having to be involved, they decided to not blow the horn but to summon individually each of those concerned. Then, he told a story of a man who used to hide in his farm whenever there was *kwii meni* in town. The headman sent a messenger to his farm and tricked him into having to do a year's porter service. Kokulah told a story about how a quarter headman tricked a friend of his by waiting on the road to his farm to recruit him for *kwii* labor. Folpah, the chief, described how he once overheard the headman being told to recruit labor for a year. He tried to hide from the headman, but the latter only wanted to share in drinking some palm wine. When he finally found Folpah, they both shared the wine, but Folpah was nervous throughout. Another of the quarter elders then told how, when he was in Salayea to visit a girlfriend, a soldier embarrassed him and later how, when he became a soldier, he got his revenge. Finally, One Day told how, once, when he was a porter, they had made a camp near a Bassa settlement. One of those he worked with stole some cassava from the Bassa. This resulted in a fight between the two, which was finally settled by all in the group having to come to his defense.

After the above pretalk, Bakolee's having left the others in his party for some personal business was formally discussed. Bakolee admitted that he was with the others in doing *kwii meni*, namely paying for an appeal in the court action initiated by Muwulu. The pretalk established the organizational grounds or *meni* meaning context as *kwii meni*. Each of the participants presented in his story a statement of his expertise in that order of reality and the responsibilities he perceived as belonging to a *kwii* person. At the conclusion of this extended preface sequence, the consequences of Bakolee's actions were clearly established. In the formal discussion that immediately followed, he apologized and offered "begging kola," in this instance, a bottle of cane juice from the town chief's shop.

The Textual Study of Secrets

Earlier I discussed how secrecy is a paradox: secrets are either told or at least constructed in such a way that they can be told. Accounts of the world are always intentionally structured according to an analyzable sequential order that can be represented by a set of formal rulelike descriptions that consist of "sets of expectations about stories, about the units of which they are composed, the way in which those units are sequenced, and the types of connections between units that are likely to occur" (Mandler, 1977:15). The text of a secret and of the lies sometimes told to conceal information are like other narrative accounts in that regard. When a lie or some fictive version of reality is used to conceal knowledge, the teller is explicitly aware of having to avoid inconsistencies that would result in the discovery that a secret is being told or alluded to.

The possession of concealed knowledge always changes the definition of the situation. McHugh (1968) describes how shifts in the definition of a situation occur through the parameters of emergence or relativity. He

claims that "emergence refers to definition, and transformation in definition, of an event over time" and relativity refers to "definition and its
transformation across space" (p. 23). The existence of secrets is relevant
to the latter. The concept of relativity holds that there are multiple
realities that can coexist at the same time (cf. Schutz, 1962). Whereas
emergence is developmental, relativity changes the meaning of events
through new perspectives. The discovery of concealed information (secrets) leads to a shift in the conception of reality, not to an understanding
of the present reality as emerging out of the old. The existence of secrets
thus reinforces the idea of alternate versions of reality. The concealed
information is the key that permits the selection of one version over the
other.

   In this chapter, I explained different ways in which concealed information is communicated to provide interpretive keys with which to differ-
entiate alternate definitions of a situation. I began by describing how
alternate accounts of the same event are intentionally structured to
provide hearers with different meanings. No one account had precedence
over the others. Instead, the significant feature of each of the versions
was the sense of the narrative. This sense was more important than the
actual events that comprised a lineal account of the case.

   This emphasis on the sense of the narrative is relevant to the interpretation of a variety of message forms that the Kpelle refer to as "deep talk." I
presented some instances of these forms to show how the narratives
analogically refer hearers to the intended sense. A primary device for
doing this is the establishment of the appropriate *meni* meaning context.
The location of organizational *meni* is the key to understanding Torkalong's account of how he became a Zo and the content of the letter telling
about the girl's disappearance from home, as well as a method for
establishing the rules of evidence and adjudicative principles for disputes
and palavers. The importance of establishing the relevant *meni* and
devices for analogically referring to alternate interpretations of reality is
especially evident in the interpretation of ritual activities. In the following
chapter, I present an account of the order of events that constituted the
initiations into the Poro that were held from 1976 to 1979.

   The same ritual act contains a variety of different meanings depending
on the membership of the interpreter and his or her right to talk within
Poro *meni*. These varying definitions of the situations and interpretations
of events are all simultaneously relevant. They are not necessarily
mutually exclusive because, as already mentioned, nonmembers and
women may know some of the "secrets" of Poro but do not possess the
same right to profess that knowledge. The methods that refer to one or
another of these alternate realities are structurally analogous to the

methods used to interpret the intended meanings of the adumbrated message forms discussed above.

The rituals presented and the talk contained within them are examined as texts in the following chapters. I demonstrate how the revealed information that is communicated changes the definition of the situation. By attending to the way interpretive keys restructure those definitions, I show how one can locate and describe the multiple versions of reality that different categories of members possess. I analyze the organization of background knowledge and shared understandings that exist between the senders and receivers of information. I identify different cohorts of members by their respective rights to know and rights to talk. Likewise, I show how people are included or excluded from knowing or professing the meanings of the rituals according to their relationship to other cohorts who also possess an equivalent right within the same organizational *meni*. This permits me to examine social networks that are defined according to the members differential access to the knowledge and interpretive keys that elicit the alternative version of the event.

6
Secrets and the Initiation Ritual

Secrecy is the substance of ritual. In the same way that secrets have renderings knowable only to those who already have knowledge of what it is to know—the so-called hermeneutical circle—rituals work simultaneously to define membership and to exclude outsiders.[1] A ritual reads something like a text. It has a narrative structure that relates ritual acts to one another across the entire process. According to Kermode (1979) there are two theories of secrecy that pertain to any religious narrative: "one says the stories are obscure on purpose to damn the outsiders; the other, even if we state it in the toughest form the language will support, says that they are not necessarily impenetrable, but that the outsiders, being what they are, will misunderstand them anyway" (p. 32). In the Poro and other societies in the complex, it is not so much a matter of not knowing the correct interpretation as not being able to profess that knowledge.

Rituals are a type of communicative genre whose meanings are described differently by the various categories of participants. In the Poro initiation rituals these include the members of the Zo hierarchy and other head elders of the society, the general membership (*tinang bia*), to-be-initiated youth (*kpulu nuu*, or in Liberian English, *sina*—"sinner") who will join at some later stage in the year-long ritual process, the Zo hierarchy of the Sande, regular members of Sande, young women who were initiated in the last initiations before the opening of the Poro initiations, young women who are not yet members of Sande, and Mandingo who will not join the Poro because of their Islamic prohibition against taking membership in non-Islamic associations.

The Ritual Drama of Initiation

The communication of Poro secrets is expressed through the visual and verbal symbolism of the numerous acts in the initiation-ritual process. That process begins when the Sande Zo turn control of the bush and town over to the Poro leadership about two years before the actual initiation period. After the bush, or "flame," is given to the men, the locations where the initiates will undergo scarification and live in a village separate from the women are fenced off and purified with a series of sacrifices. During this time, family members attempt to resolve any palavers or disputes so that they can be unified during the ritual process.

The period of initiation begins with the entry into the Poro bush of a member of the Zo family who is called the *Folpah* and the eldest nonmember son of the *loi kalong*, or landlord, followed by a number of other initiates who are older than most others entering during the year, for this first group is responsible for building the initiation village for those that join throughout the year. The joint entry of the *Folpah* and the *loi kalong*'s son represents a uniting of both the sacred and the secular parts of the community. The first group to enter is usually quite large. Their ritual of entry is essentially the same as for all others who follow them over the course of the year, except for the very last groups that enter only a few weeks before the end of the initiation period. The latter groups also engage in the same rituals, but they are much shorter in length, and there is less attention paid to the initiates when they are taken into the fence.

In the entry ritual, initiates are first "captured" by the *kwelebah*, or Zo nephew, who ties a thatch sash, called a *japa*, around each of them. The *japa* signifies that they are now initiates and that no woman can come near them while they are in the community. The initiates' fathers or other sponsors in the society present them with wooden swords, usually dipped in chicken blood. They are told to kill the *ngamu* with the swords and are asked which part of the devil they will carry back to town. They are then led throughout the community to visit the homes of various male relatives, who present them with head ties, which are put on them. That night they sleep in a specially chosen house for initiates and are given a hot meal and a bath the next morning. They are then led throughout the town, presented to the *loi kalong* and the Zo responsible for the new initiates, and led out of town to the Poro fence in the bush. There, the *ngamu* peformer is waiting. The boys are stripped to the waists and led through the forest to the area of the initiation village. Just before entering the village, the boys are taken to a stream, where they are scarred on their necks, chests, and backs. These scars are considered the teeth marks of the devil.

When the boys reach the area where scarification takes place, the *kwelebah* returns to the community and, in a ritual called *juanay*, announces that the boys are dead. Before his appearance, the women dance with tense movements and chant "Carry them and bring them back." The *kwelebah* runs into the community ringing a bell. The women immediately cease their songs and follow him around the town, shouting jubilantly. After entering each of the quarters, the *kwelebah* returns to the forest. He goes to the area where the boys are undergoing scarification and waits there until the scarring of the last initiate is completed. He then returns to town, accompanied by most of the men who carried the initiates into the area. At that, the initiates are permitted to enter into the bush community. Their wounds are rubbed with clay. They are not permitted to wear shirts for the entire duration of their stay.

Before reaching town, the men who accompany the *kwelebah* stop and pick a particular leaf that contains a red latex that signifies the blood of the initiates. Running behind the *kwelebah*, they enter the town, then stop in each quarter and form into a circle, chanting *kanokowai*, which means "The devil has given birth to you." As they pass through the town, the men toss their leaves on top of the houses of the initiates' families or give portions to other men who did not accompany the boys that day, in return for a small token or drink of cane juice. When the men are finished, groups of women from each *taa*, or moiety, dance the *jinja* dance. They wear shell anklets that make a percussion sound as they dance in a circle. There is no musical accompaniment other than the sound of the shells.

These rituals are performed each Monday throughout the year-long initiation period. The only initiations that do not follow this pattern are those of reluctant youth or children from families who cannot afford the large family feast that is given after the *kanokowai* ritual is completed. Those boys are taken into the forest at night by the *Baiyaemu* devil discussed previously. At the conclusion of the year, the last boy to enter into the forest is the son of a Zo, called the *Zomu*. It is this family that closes the bush. After the *Zomu* enters, no one else can join. His entry ritual is similar to that of the other initiates except that no other boys enter the bush with him.

During the week the *Zomu* is in the bush, there are several feasts in the initiation village. Finally, at the completion of the initiation period, the *ngamu* enters town, exposing itself to both members and nonmembers. It visits each of the quarters, announcing that in the evening its wife will deliver. That evening the pregnancy is theatrically enacted while nonmembers are behind closed doors. The boys are taken from the bush village to a fenced area outside of the community called *luwaa*, or the washing fence. Just before they enter the area, the *ngamu* announces their new names (which have actually been given them before this ritual). The devil selects those boys from the major families to represent all the other initiates in the naming ritual. He first calls them by unacceptable names, such as Worm, Caterpillar, and Sucro (the mountain). The father of each boy refuses each name until the *ngamu* calls the correct one. After several of the boys are given names, the entire group is led into the washing fence. At that, their fathers announce to the boys' mothers that they are reborn and tell of the new names. Everyone in the community celebrates until sunrise.

The next day, the women are permitted to carry bath water and hot food to the front of the washing fence, which members then carry in to the boys, who bathe, eat, and put on full-length gowns and long caps decoratively covered with safety pins. Near sunset, the boys are led into the town in a long procession headed by the *Folpah* and are taken to their respective quarters, where they sit on mats. They are not permitted to speak unless spoken to by their families or the Zo. It is at this time that the women are permitted to walk up and down the lines of initiates to search for their children. They are allowed to greet the boys but cannot interact with them to any extent. Mothers of very young children are permitted at that time to take them into their homes, however, as these children are not expected to participate any longer in the events that follow. That night, the initiates are taken by their quarter elders into secluded parts of the community, where they sleep together in groups within their respective quarters. The next morning, they are taken to the *loi kalong* by the *kwelebah* and formally presented to him. Gifts are exchanged between the chief and the Zo, and the *loi kalong* pays tribute to the families of initiates that came to Sucromu to have their kinsmen join. After the *loi kalong* accepts the initiates, they return to their *kolii*. The Zo then dance through the community in their last procession, and accept tribute from each family in the town.

In the evening the town is turned over to the initiates for parties. Most of the adult community goes to bed early that night. The young girls dress in their finest *lappa* and dresses for an evening of dancing and sometimes lovemaking with the new initiates. Although the boys are permitted to interact with all members of the community, they are still required to wear their hats for a week. During this period, their fathers or other sponsors in the society present them to their *ngala* and other relatives, where they receive gifts of food, drink, and clothing. Finally, the *Zomu* removes his hat in the presence of his father and his eldest *ngala*. After that, all of the other initiates can remove their hats and return to a normal life.

The Operation of Ritual Metaphors

Earlier I discussed how members from certain categories may possess identical knowledge but not have the same rights to "talk it." What is *ifa mo* for one group may be expressed by another. For instance, a member of the Poro may refer to the place where the novices reside as *weiawoli* (the "little forest") or euphemistically as Nairobi, after the capital of Kenya, which is popular in Liberia because of its Highlife recordings.[2] The women, however, must openly maintain that the boys are dead and living in the *ngamu ko su* ("inside the devil's stomach"). Both the men and women know that the boys reside in the bush community, but whereas the men can directly refer to that information, the women must practice *ifa mo* and not mention it. If a woman should openly discuss what she knows, she may be killed for the infraction, the case of Kapu allegedly being one such instance. If the Poro Zo decide that the woman can in the future still be trusted, they may force her to become an assistant to the *tipinenu*, or woman member of the society, rather than suffer death. During the last initiation, two women were placed in this category after they accidently witnessed some internal Zo activity. When a woman talks about the boys, she must do so using the ritual metaphors that comprise the symbolic vocabulary of the initiation process; namely, the boys were killed in a battle with the *ngamu*, are presently living in its stomach, and will be reborn in an elaborate "pregnancy" ritual involving the *Malangawlaw ngamunea* type of devil's wife.

There are always two forms that the Poro secrets take: that which is known but cannot be talked (the substance of the secret whose direct formulation constitutes an exposure, especially for those who do not have the right to profess) and that which can be spoken (the metaphorical expression of the secret). The latter includes all the indirect message forms, including ritual, through which concealed knowledge is expressed. Although the women know that the boys are really alive and thus assign an epistemological priority to the real, rather than the ritual, reality, if one of the boys should die during his liminal period of residence in the bush community, the women can only discuss the death using the symbolic language of ritual metaphor.

In the Poro and the other associations discussed earlier, there are two types of rituals that can be distinguished: rituals of illusion and rituals of allusion. Both involve the articulation of verbal and visual symbols during performance. Rituals of illusion are those in which participants produce auditory or visual manifestations or both such as the different kinds of devils, the various malefic spirits (*jina*), witches (*wulu nuu*) of the Mina society, and ancestral spirits (*gawfaw*) that are controlled by the Moling. Belief in the reality of these various theatrically produced illusions depends on one's membership in the secret societies, as well as on the grade of membership held within each of them, as can be seen when comparing beliefs about the *ngamu* with those about the ancestral spirits that intervene in daily life. Most people realize that the *ngamu* is actually one of the Poro members wearing the mask and costume, but only those of high Poro grade and the Zo know how to perform the role and precisely how the devil exercises its powers. Although every member and even most of the nonmembers know that the *ngamu* is theatrically performed and who is acting its role, an illusion of a real and powerful creature, independent of that production, is created. In contrast, very few nonmembers share with the leaders of the Moling the belief that the appearances of the ancestral spirits in the town are actually illusions theatrically performed by the society's membership, for this is knowledge normally gained upon initiation into the association. Because only those of high status are usually able to afford the costly Moling initiation fee, this knowledge is the possession of but an elite cohort within the community. Some nonmembers believe throughout their lives that ancestors actually appear corporally in the community. In any case, it is only the members of Moling that can profess the knowledge that the spirits are performed. Learning that ancestral spirits are really illusions produced similarly to the *ngamu* (and *wulu nuu* in the Mina) does not destroy a new Moling member's belief in Kpelle cosmology. Rather, new initiates have an even stronger sense of responsibility for maintaining the public belief system by referring to the spirit apparitions as real.

Rituals of allusion are similar to what Turner (1974) and Fernandez (1977) have each called "ritual metaphors." These are ritual acts whose interpretations analogically refer participants to other definitions of the event. Both members and nonmembers recognize that the symbols displayed differ from what is asserted during their production. An example is the white chalk the new initiates wear rubbed over their faces and bodies after they leave the initiation village and reenter the community. The meaning of the chalk was expressed to me by one informant, who claimed:

> The fact is to distinguish them from us. Anyone can wear the gown; it is to distinguish them. They are the newly born. Like when you born a new baby you put powder on the person. So that is just what they do. They are the newly born people.

Likewise, the rebirth is not an illusion that the boys are actually brought back to life through the womb of *Malangawlaw ngamunea*. This female devil is used instead to *allude* to the new status of the initiates. The pregnancy is an allusion inasmuch as the nonmembers already share in the knowledge that the boys have really been brought to town and are in a line just outside of town behind the specially constructed fence, later to be led into the community as the "newly born."

In both rituals of illusion and rituals of allusion, the event has the structural form of a secret. It is a kind of adumbrated message form for expressing concealed information. Rituals demonstrate their textual character when participants as well as those who witness a given performance are able to describe what occurred with any one of several formulations. This is especially evident when members discuss differences in practices or divergencies in the order of ritual acts between neighboring communities. The they-do-it-differently comparison is a member's formal recognition of the ritual's narrative form. There is, nevertheless, an essential difference between rituals as texts and other narrative forms.

Both spoken and written texts result in messages that are denotatively understood. They are composed of structurally interrelated themes that are sequentially arranged across the course of the narrative. Specific protagonists are identified who engage in a series of episodic adventures that contain the kinds of functions identified by analysts of oral tradition: the recognition of conflict, the setting of goals, attempts to satisfy them, and eventual resolution (Arewa and Shreve, 1975). Rituals, on the other hand, do not result in the same kinds of formulations as spoken narratives. They share with myths and other stories a set of event schemata implicatively related to one another, and these schemata may be either sequentially ordered or embedded within each other.[3] When stories are remembered, they are usually summarized to gloss over certain episodes and embedded schemata while attending to others. The speakers' choice of which schemata to explicate, gloss over, treat as tangential, or ignore involves the intentional ordering of the remembered story in the sequence of other stories told within the interactional setting. Likewise, when rituals are remembered, some acts are remembered as focal and tangential while others are glossed over and ignored. But questions such as the meaning of the ritual involve interpretations that are more than simple summaries of what occurred. Respondents recognize an analogical character to ritual acts, for the acts refer to external realities separate from the events that made up their performance.

The referred-to realities are different for the various categories of participants, so a ritual act may have several meanings; yet it is always recognized as being in a sequentially appropriate position in the order of performance. In this way, rituals share properties in common with other types of secrecy message forms. As discussed earlier, when concealed information is communicated in an adumbrated manner, the key is relevant only to a selected membership cohort. All others not part of that group are, nevertheless, able to interpret meanings for the speech act that served as the key. For these others, the act is sequentially appropriate in the discussion even though they do not have the background knowledge necessary to use the act as a key. When lies are used to conceal information, they concomitantly reveal to others who share in that knowledge that a secret is being hidden through subterfuge. Thus, the lie, as a text, is the interpretive key for those who share in the hidden knowledge. Both the adumbrated speech act and the intentional lie are thus similar to ritual acts that are understood differently by the categories of participants.

Members of the Moling and Mina use the respective lies that *gawfaw* and *wulu nuu* appear in the community as a method for discriminating between members and nonmembers. These lies are keys for interpreting the narrative production of the societies' rituals. When the lies are shared by both members and nonmembers, as in the initiation ritual, they adumbrate the referred-to reality. Nonmembers are constrained to use the lies, whereas members have a choice between the lies and more direct forms of expression. The women share with the men the knowledge that the initiates are not really dead, but living instead in the forest, to be brought back to the community later in the ritual process. The concealed information is not what is consequential in this case; rather, it is the process of keeping secrets through the recognition of one's right to talk and one's speaking prerogative relative to all others present during a social encounter. The initiations provide the women with a type of instruction in how to practice secrecy (as do the Sande initiation rituals for the men). These instructions are implicitly gained by the women both in their position as knowledgeable observers during the men's performances (where they are constrained in the ways they can publicly discuss those acts) and in the course of their own rituals, which complement those of the men.

The following is an example of songs the women sing as they dance in procession about the community in celebration of the entrance of the boys into the Poro fence earlier in the day. The song reveals an awareness of the boys' fate without ever explicitly mentioning the information. Each line of the song is followed first by a translation into Liberian English, then by a paraphrase.

Jina dalii aa pElEn kele long
Men are gone with house sweeping child
[The men carried away the house sweeper]

Ku kE galaw aa hoya
We used to see as a joke

[We used to think of it as a joke]

Long lii he jinaa koi
Child heart not men stomach
[Men do not have feelings for a child]

jina kele hiyima wo ka
Men every agreement [or join] talk [this] is
[This is an agreement reached by all men]

Nyanbe meni pawlaw kula joe kaie
I have matter original take-out [unfolds] Zo in my hand
[I have a Zo that can reveal original matters]

Bele aa pene aa wanlanwanlan
The play [performance or ritual] has changed to seriousness
[The play has become serious]

Wele kelen ngon tolaa walaa
Song hot [as a state of being] to sing strong
[It is hard to sing a hot song]

Jinaa dali aa nloi namu long
Men are gone with landowner child
[The men have gone away with the landowner's child]

Long lElE ponon kayea
Child good substitute in my hand
[I have a good child to substitute]

Nuu ngai lawwa malan ngan
Person face is just friend face
[A person's face is just his friend's face]

The song demonstrates knowledge that the initiates are not, as the ritual metaphors assert, dead. It instead recognizes that the boys are in the men's custody and expresses the mothers' concern about the general callousness of men toward children ("men do not have feelings for a child"). The boys' departure from the community is attributed to "an agreement reached by all the men" as revealed by the "Zo that can reveal original matters." Before the initiations, there is a great deal of joking and teasing of the initiates about their having to do battle with the devil (an example is presented in the next chapter). What is initially a joke is, in the song, recognized as serious ("the play has become serious"). The town chief, as the owner of the land, is given respect in the lines about substituting the singers' children for his own. The ability to substitute one boy for another derives from the prior practice of substituting poorer or lower status townsmen during time of war. The fact that "a person's face is just his friend's face" asserts how one is as good as another.

When the boys leave their mothers, they become men. In their singing, the women recognize that their children are still alive. Because the open expression of this knowledge would be an exposure of the Poro secrets, the women communicate through innuendo and oblique reference. The songs provide a type of instruction in how to practice secrecy. The method is reaffirmed for the old members and made explicit for the women recently initiated into the Sande during the last initiation rituals. That group of women is recognized as a separate cohort throughout the Poro initiations and is required to leave town when the boys are "reborn" and enter into the community at the end of the ritual process.

The secrets of the Poro rituals are not defined in terms of content because the women share with the men much of what is concealed during the initiation period. What is important are the procedures for knowing how to communicate protected information while being recognized by all others as practicing the *ifa mo* proscription. These techniques are both artful and circumscribed. The numerous symbols used in the rituals shift in their references; consequently, there are different methods for interpreting and using them. Not only does a given ritual act have a set of divergent ways in which its meaning is formulated, but it changes in meaning according to its appearance in the sequence of other acts during the year-long ritual process. This is significant for the delineation of the sociology of knowledge for the rituals, which is based on the distribution of information among members according to their socially stratified position within the community. The Poro initiations demonstrate how the same information may be held by different categories of members, the methods of expression varying rather than the content.

The ways in which symbols change in reference and the manner in which they can be articulated by the categories of members are evident in the examination of the following interview with an informant I shall call Flumo. I asked him for an account of the history and organization of the Poro along with his interpretation of the events performed during the stages of the ritual process. As his answer involved descriptions relevant to most of the issues addressed in this chapter, I present our conversation in full.

An Interview about the Poro

FLUMO: The Poro society began in the eighteenth century, and then it came over to Liberia. When it first came to Liberia, it came around the Loma area.

BLB: What were the first people who had Poro?

FLUMO: Well, the Loma and Kpelle in Guinea. That is where it all started from, O.K., and then from there it came over to the Gbandi people almost at the border of Sierra Leone. From there, it came over this way now, to the area here. But the main reason why it stopped in Guinea is that there is a town called Zoglomee. Zoglomee, there is a town there where they were having the bush, the bush society. And then the people, the boys in the society bush and the Zo, took a pregnant lady and killed her. So, one day things came up, and they collected every one of them and even the devil, the one that they close the door, the horn they blow at night, everything. They called them in the market grounds and in a wide place had them demonstrate what they do at night. And from that time the president [Sékou Touré] put a stop to it in Guinea. That is why everybody comes to Liberia to really take part in the Poro society. There is no longer a system there.

BLB: Why did they kill the woman?

FLUMO: They killed the woman in Zoglomee.

BLB: Do you know for what reason they killed her?

FLUMO: They killed her to make (coughs), to fix some medicine. To make some medicine so that they can make the business so high that the medicine would work harder. Is just the reason why they killed her.

BLB: Do they ever do things like that here in Liberia?

FLUMO: In Liberia? Just a couple weeks ago I heard something like that in a Loma town behind Bablazo. There the people burned a little girl. Even a couple police from here went there to arrest the people. They got a little girl. They went and made a fire. They burned that person. They have done it three times there. This time they caught them.

BLB: Why did they burn them?

FLUMO: They burned them to fix medicine. So they caught the people, that they are still waiting to hear more. I don't know what the people are going to say about it. Even in Liberia they can stop it no more. That happened in Liberia once.

BLB: What is the meaning of burning someone?

FLUMO: There is not just one. It has so many meanings. Certain medicines that the people want, that anything they say should be the truth. They should have the final [i.e., major] reason. So that is why they do such, uh, that is why they do some of those things.

BLB: What about the man who they wanted to burn here? The one who committed suicide?

FLUMO: Oh the man who killed himself here. He as for his own, the reason why the people didn't want to bury him good is that he killed himself. On traditionally [according to tradition] no one killed him. He killed himself, so the people had to get rid of him. In fact they were not to bury him with clothes. But they did bury him with clothes. The clothes that were on him they were to take off and then just bury him like that. Because he never wanted life this way.

BLB: Is there a meaning to why they take the clothes off?

FLUMO: Oh the meaning is that he just don't want to enjoy his life now. He is tired with the earth. So he need not carry anything from here.

BLB: Let me ask you about the boy, Yakpawolo's brother, who is going to be the last to go in now. How was he selected to be the last person to be initiated?

FLUMO: In the community you will have a special person who is the son of a Zo. His children are always the last. And then they are the ones that can close. Sunday the other people will go. Monday the little boy will go. And when he goes no one else will go. He is called the *Zomu*.

BLB: And who is the first to go in?

FLUMO: There is not a particular one person. There were twelve that went in one day. And there was one boy who they used to call Peter, but now is called Kpulmo. He was the biggest among them.

BLB: When do they do the naming?

FLUMO: They will do the naming later in town. They will bring them here, and when they bring them, they will call their names. When they call their names at that time, they will say the devil will deliver. And while the devil delivers, now they will start calling the names out. After calling the names, they will all come in town. But that will happen right in town. But we know their names now. When we visit them, we know their names now. When we visit them, we know their names.

BLB: How were they given the names there?

FLUMO: They give names according to the position they do. According to the position. The activity you are taking part in. A kind of job you are major in, they got names for that.

BLB: What are the kinds of jobs that exist?

FLUMO: Well, like a lower place here . . . the Kpasa Gissi where I visited the last time when seventy-nine persons went into the society bush, there they have a blacksmith kitchen. They have some weavers, servers, and other things; you know, when you are a blacksmith you take the name of your boss. But here there is nothing like that. There is no blacksmith kitchen, nothing. There are some other activities, like some people who sing on the devil. The man who sings on the devil at night and you hear it. He will have an assistant from there, and that person will carry his name. Like the *kwelebah* who can be running around. He has an assistant there, and he will carry his name. Kwelebah, too. You see. And so forth just like that.

BLB: How about everybody else's name? Let's say, uh, Bakolleah.

FLUMO: Bakolleah and kwelebah are the same thing.

BLB: Uh, let's say Folpah.

FLUMO: Folpah, they have so many Folpah, but the main Folpah is the one when they take them out you will see him. He is the biggest of all. He is a Zo. Folpah is the Zo. Of all the Zo of all the boys, he will be the head. He is the *Folpah*.

BLB: Like Folpahzoi was the *Folpah*?

FLUMO: Yes, he was the *Folpah*, so he is the big man. Folpahzoi, he is a big Zo.

BLB: Will he be the one who will take the boys out of the bush?

FLUMO: No, when they take them out, this man will be the one that will present them to Vallai [the landlord or chief]. A *Folpah* is the one who will lead his people from the bush into the town. But not Folpahzoi. There is a *Folpah* there now. His name is Sudeah.

BLB: All right, but the other boys who carry the name Folpah, how do they get that name?

FLUMO: That name, they just get it. The namesake [*doma*]. Like I am Folpah too, and someone wants to get my name Folpah, but that doesn't mean for a special job or I will do a special thing. They have only a special one person. Like the day they got Gwiiboy. So many Gwiiboy, but they got one Gwiiboy, who is the Zo. The *Gwiiboy* for all. [Flumo is saying that some of those who have the Folpah or Gwiiboy names are officers in the society, while others are given those names at the request of their families.]

BLB: For the women?

FLUMO: Yes. Like we have Kwelebah; she is the only Gwiiboy here.

BLB: What is the name of the woman who is in the society?

FLUMO: In both the men and woman? They call her Tipe. She join both man and woman. She can visit there.

BLB: Is she considered a Zo?

FLUMO: She is a Zo. She be a she is a Zo.

BLB: So a woman who does that, she always goes by the same name?

FLUMO: Yes, but they got another name, she got her natural name or artificial name that she got. She will be known like that. Tipe. But they don't call her that way out so everybody can call her.

BLB: I want to get a chronology of what happens throughout the year. The boys who first went into the bush, they were the ones who made the forest, the camp itself. Right?

FLUMO: Um, the camp before they go there, a couple of little huts there. A couple of little ones.

BLB: Who builds the houses?

FLUMO: All the members do that. We even make a farm there.

BLB: All right, and then the first boys go in. First they are taken by the *kwelebah* and taken around the town. And then into the bush. They go behind that fence and are taken to the waterside, and that is where they put the scars on them.

FLUMO: Yes, all that is correct.

BLB: Is there any special meaning to the scars?

FLUMO: The only meaning for it is that this thing equal that they got a sign of respect and the society. It is just like the UBF [United Brotherhood Fellowship—a modern-sector secret association]. You join and they put a mark on you. The scar shows that you are a member of it. It shows that everybody that you are a member of it. That is why they put it all the way even where the shirt can notice it here, or they make it come here [by the neck] so that you can see it. So that they can see that you are a member.

BLB: All right, but someone also explained that, for example, the scars on the back of the neck are supposed to be the marks of the devil—you know, the devil's teeth on the neck. Is that right?

FLUMO: Uh, that is the mark of the devil, that is the mark of the devil. Whenever the devil eating you like that, you see the devil eat you.

BLB: Is that put on at the same time as the scars on the body?

FLUMO: Everything is done at the same time. They finish with it in one day. It is like something like a hook. They hold it with a little knife. They fold it so and cut it off.

BLB: What is the name of the person who does that?

FLUMO: The person, there are so many of them that can do that. I know several that are trying to practice it there. It is just that I cannot make it with human blood; it get me somehow I don't know.

BLB: Is there a special name for that office? Does the person who does it go by a special name?

FLUMO: A certain name? No, even a man like Gotojui [a respected town elder who is not part of the Zo family]. Folpahzoi can do it.

BLB: So, you don't call them by a particular name?

FLUMO: No, no they don't call them like that. They just call them *ngamu*. They are the devil.

BLB: All right, and from there the first group of men that is with the *kwelebah* goes back into town.

FLUMO: They go there before they get through cutting. They will come, and they bring what they call *juanay*. O.K., when they come, then later the *kwelebah* go; then we all get leaves now and come in town. That shows that the devil has killed the person.

BLB: What is the song that they sing?

FLUMO: *Zoxana kokway, kokway.*

BLB: What does it mean?

FLUMO: Uh, it means that the Zo has reborn you; the Zo has reborn me.

BLB: And then they throw the leaves on the houses?

FLUMO: Yes and give the rest to people.

BLB: From the place where the boys are scarred, they go directly into the bush village?

FLUMO: The camp is just like here, and here the devil eats them. And from there he goes in town.

BLB: Is there a special name for the camp?

FLUMO: Oh there is not special name. It is just what we call it in town. In town itself, we don't have a special name for it. If you see some people, we say, "I am going to Nairobi." Most of the older people call it *weiawoli, weiawoli* [the "little forest"].

BLB: And when the boys go there, what do they do?

FLUMO: When they go there now, they just stay there and learn different things. Like how the devil *eayeah* [in imitation of the devil's song]. The *eayeah* name of the devil, they can sing it in the night, that all in the night. There are some who know how to blow their thing for sounds to sing behind the devil. Some people learn how to dance in the devil; that is the dancing devil that comes out.

BLB: So there is no sp. . . there are several different people that can wear the devil's costume?

FLUMO: There are some people—yeah—there are some people who learn how to do the same thing, the devil to eat, how the devil eat person and like that.

BLB: What are they called?

FLUMO: The people who do that? Oh, they are the devil.

BLB: And the persons who sing behind the devil are *pene wo* [translators]?

FLUMO: Yes. They learn many things there. Like singing, like dancing devil, all like that. The eating of the devil, the eating someone, how usually they do the dance. Some of them learn that. Some of them learn talking, how the devil talk, they learn that.

BLB: How is that done?

FLUMO: You know what the devil sounds like. Just like that. And they throw sign like that.

BLB: How about the laws of medicine?

FLUMO: Yea. Some people learn some other job, some other medicine business, too.

BLB: What other kinds of medicine business do they do?

FLUMO: Some people learn, uh, some of these kinds of things. Those that are the Zo, those who are the Zo, the children of the Zo that are not attending, who are not going to school [the public school], they go under another workshop under someone. Some of these big, big people, these big, big Zo. And they start learning those leaf medicines, those small, small medicines. So when that person dies, that person will replace him.

BLB: What kinds of medicines does the Poro have?

FLUMO: The kind of medicine. There is no certain medicine that the Poro has. No special medicine.

BLB: Like, for example, in the Snake Society you learn specific medicines for snakebites, and you also learn medicines to call snakes—

FLUMO: No, no, no the Poro society is not such a thing. Like me, I don't know any other leaf to say that I know medicine. Ya, just go in there to be initiated, to be member, that is all. The devil come out, you go there. The only medicine they have is the devil.

BLB: Don't they also have medicines to protect the community, to have war medicines—

FLUMO: Those medicines are medicines with those Zo, medicines with those Zo. Like my old Pa, he has some medicines he can protect the house no witch, no suffer, no bad thing should happen here. He kill chicken on it sometimes. You see, that is all.

BLB: I was told that there are certain laws that, let's say, if you are walking in the bush like this and someone comes this side, that you always go to one side and you do not split up into two sides and let the person pass between you. I was told that was a law of Poro.

FLUMO: Yes.

BLB: What other kinds of laws are there?

FLUMO: Like for a typical example, if I go back there and I get there, any of those boys see me, they have to bend down until I pass.

That is the respect and the training they undergo. Two, when you are walking on the road and you find someone coming and you people are two walking, you go one side and they pass one side; they shouldn't pass between you because the person that has the bad luck carrying and he passes between you, it will stay on you. You see, these are the things. The next thing for respect, again because they are more likely teaching that they have to respect people on it, those are some of the things. If you see someone coming with a load on their head, you excuse the person's pass; you don't allow the person to get into the bush; you go to the side of the road and the person passes. And then you get there.

BLB: And what other kinds of things do they learn for respect?

FLUMO: The kind of things for respect? Like if I see any of my elder, some old Pa, uh, and I want to shake their hand, I take off my hat and I shake the person's hand. You see I don't leave the hat on and shake the person's hand. You see only a Poro man should do that. Like a typical example, when I am sitting, I see any of the old people coming, I get up and let them sit down. I am supposed to stand. When we are eating, I am supposed to hold the can with my hand and we eat.

BLB: Let me give you a case of something. Do you know Nuita?

FLUMO: Yea.

BLB: Well, he was getting into a lot of trouble in town. Like he would steal a chicken and kill it and things like that. And he was just giving people a lot of palaver. So, they put him in the bush, and they said that they put him there because he will learn not to do those kinds of things. How would they give him instruction about not being bad?

FLUMO: Some of the instruction is that when he is there they are going to train him. One, sometime everyday they will put him under the sun, bind him down, lay down under the sun there. All right, two, because he is around there, there is nothing that he will see to steal, and if he makes the attempt to steal something, well when they get over him they will punish him to the dead. There is nothing for him to run around; there is nothing he can do, and nobody can fight the devil. So anything the boys want to do with him, they will do with him. So that means he will get changed.

BLB: What kinds of things have they done to him?

FLUMO: The very first thing that they did to him was that when the devil was ready to eat him, the man who went there he was— sometimes they act bad, the man would start easy, slowly, you

know, the pain; the pain will hurt the person too much. And
sometimes when the sun is hot, that is the time they do such.
The devil start eating slowly, slowly. And when they are finished
all around here, and when you move from there, the next time
they tell you "Don't do this," you can't do it. It can hurt.

BLB: So far have all the boys survived? Have any of the boys died in
the bush?

FLUMO: No, no, no, nothing. They are all living. Nothing happen to
them there. None of them is sick, nothing. No trouble again.

BLB: I heard that if a boy gets sick before he comes out, they might
not allow him to come out.

FLUMO: Well, since this is the modern days now, they don't do it. If
the person gets sick, the nurse goes there. D.M. [the nurse who
runs the clinic outside of Sucromu] and the other one go there
and treat the person. If it gets critical, they go to Zorzor and get
somebody to treat it.

BLB: But in the old times they might not let the person live?

FLUMO: Oh, in the old days, even in our days if we suffer a lot, we
took—actually—they—after the devil finish eating you and they
go and put you on a *kinja* [thatch basket], put some leaves there,
and tie you up. You stay there until the sore gets some kind of
way [scabs], and then they take you from there. If you see others
can conquer, but this time it is nothing, they don't take *kinja* this
time, after from there they just give them injection. That's
finished with that.

BLB: So, they are giving them injections now?

FLUMO: Yes.

BLB: Have they been doing any schooling there for any of the boys?
Like teaching them how to read.

FLUMO: No.

BLB: Right now there are about a thousand people there. What kinds
of things are they doing during the day? What is a typical day
like? I know they are not learning things all of the time.

FLUMO: Some of them are not even learning because there are small
children there. Like even some of them cannot even walk good.
They are there now.

BLB: Who cooks for them?

FLUMO: The older boys cook. They do everything. They gather
materials; the older boys cook. They [the small children] are just
there to play. In fact the town is big now. It is a large town. It is
very enjoyable. Most of them don't even want to come [out]
now. Every day they got food to eat. No suffer, nothing.

BLB: And palm wine and things like that?

FLUMO: Everything.

BLB: Let me ask you. When the boys come out, they are going to march, then, through the town, and they will go to the . . . they will go by the cottonwood tree outside of town, right?

FLUMO: They will pass at night.

BLB: Will that be closed doors?

FLUMO: Closed doors. And the devil will go back, and it will stay long. It will call and it will deliver. So the devil born.

BLB: And they stay there one day?

FLUMO: One day.

BLB: And what is the washing fence?

FLUMO: They go there after the devil deliver. That is the place they will wash, bathe them, and put white chalk on them.

BLB: When they come to town, they come in with bowed heads?

FLUMO: Yes, everyone of them will bow. It is hard to see their faces.

BLB: After they are in town, they will still wear their gowns for a week or so?

FLUMO: Oh yes, after they finish they will present them to their own parents; then, then everybody will be playing to their houses and so forth. They will be wearing their gowns for weeks. Every morning they bathe and go make something on it [i.e., put medicine leaves into water]. In fact, they will spend—some of those ladies used to spend some by us—they will spend a couple of days without even talking to a lady.

BLB: Is there a special name for that period?

FLUMO: There is no special name. It is just that they have taken them out. The newly born people.

BLB: When the boys are in the bush, they are in the devil's stomach?

FLUMO: Yes, in the stomach of the devil. Even things that we carry, we say that we are carrying it to the devil. Like biscuit, bread, and what we say is that we are carrying it to the devil.

BLB: What are the boys allowed to wear?

FLUMO: Only trousers, no shirt. They use chalk on them.

BLB: And what do they sleep on?

FLUMO: They sleep on a mat, no blanket. Those are the training they are taking. You don't cover yourself. You must go around without shirt.

BLB: Can they drink cane juice?

FLUMO: Some of them drink it, but you hide it. Like you hide it and carry it, you call the person in the bush and sit down. The person drinks it. Even cigarette you smoke there; there is a law that nobody carry cigarette there. Nobody find it with you, you are in trouble. But we carry it there anyway; we hide it and carry it.

BLB: But the boys are allowed to tap palm wine?

FLUMO: Yes. They can do that. They can do all sorts of things. Some even cut hair. In fact I might go there for a haircut.

BLB: Does the devil often come out where the boys are?

FLUMO: They themselves are doing everything. They have learned everything.

BLB: So now when the devil comes to town, it is the boys?

FLUMO: Yes. Those bigger ones, they are the ones who learn it. They are about eight; those that dance are about ten.

BLB: When the devil comes into town at night, do all the boys follow?

FLUMO: Not all of them; they bring about ten or fifteen of them.

BLB: When they come to town, what do they do?

FLUMO: They go around with us.

BLB: I want to ask something we talked before. When the *kwelebah* comes into town ringing the bell and the men run behind him, what do they sing?

FLUMO: When they come in town with the leaf?

BLB: No, during the *juanay*.

FLUMO: They sing that all the bad things that was on the person, that they carry, everything is running away. They say all the things that you are doing is running away [*di pe de pu je zua nea*].

BLB: Like if he was a bad person . . .

FLUMO: Yes, we can get a good action from the person now. Then they go back and bring the leaves. When they come, they sing *kanekwoykwey, kwoykwey*.

BLB: Do you know why so many men from Guinea are coming here to join the society?

FLUMO: The reason why is that, although they don't carry into the system there, but they have some other fact, some other things, sometime they are ready to divide something, they say that no nonmember can go there. I am not member, those the things. Members can go there, nonmember cannot go. So they cannot join there, and they try to come here. [Flumo is saying that they do not have the Poro "system" in Guinea but that they still have the society (thus *system* refers to initiation). Whenever Poro members in Guinea want to share something, nonmembers cannot go near. Thus, to participate, they must go to Liberia to join the society.]

BLB: How far do you think the people are traveling?

FLUMO: Oh, some of them a whole day's walk. Even now the people have gone to walk, they have soldiers all around the border. They don't want the people to leave there and come. So the people find a lot of hard time. They pass through the bush. Struggle, struggle until they can cross.

BLB: So even though they don't practice the society, they use it to have their secret meetings?

FLUMO: Yes, that is why the government is afraid.

BLB: But they also have other kinds of societies there?

FLUMO: The same society like Mina, Moling, and like that.

BLB: Then why would a person need to join Poro?

FLUMO: If you are not a member of Poro, you cannot join Mina. And some other society, only Moling you can join. So that is why they come here, so they can join that.

BLB: Do they tell you the story of creation, how the world got created and how man got born?

FLUMO: In the Poro?

BLB: Yes, do they learn those things?

FLUMO: No, no, no. Those are not the things we learn in Poro. I already told you about it.

BLB: Do you know anything of the history of the society?

FLUMO: That is just what I narrated and why it broke up in Guinea. That is the reason, the murder of the pregnant lady.

As Flumo was repeating information, I ended the interview with the normal polite closings and the sharing of kola (drinking cane juice).

Reference and Meaning Shifts

Flumo proffered different referents for the initiation-ritual metaphors according to their sequential appearance in the overall ritual process. These meaning shifts corresponded to whether the symbols appeared in rituals of illusion or rituals of allusion. To understand these differences, I turn to some considerations of the nature of metaphor in general and how it applies to our understanding of ritual events.[4]

Ricouer (1977) argues that once metaphor becomes incorporated into language, it ceases to be creative and consequently is no longer what he refers to as a "living metaphor." It is, in his words, "dead." The meanings of so-called dead metaphors are polysemic; that is, they are coterminous definitions of the term. Take for example, the word *rat*. Its primary dictionary definition in the nominal case refers to any one of a number of rodents that differ from mice in their size and dentition. The secondary meanings are "a contemptible person, as a betrayer, scab, or informer" and also "a pad over which a woman's hair is arranged." Although the secondary meanings may once have been metaphoric extensions of the first, they are now so much a part of the term that they do not add anything new to our perception or understanding of the referred-to object. This understanding of dead metaphors has implications for the analysis of ritual.

Following Ricouer (1977), the multiple interpretations of ritual symbols can only be alternative renderings similar to the extended dictionary definitions of figurative vocabulary entities, for there are no new meanings added to those that existed before the symbol's appearance in the ritual. For Ricouer, true metaphor is "the rhetorical process by which discourse unleashes the power that certain fictions have to re-describe reality" (p. 7). Ritual symbols do not so much redescribe reality as refer to already established definitions of it. Instead of being true metaphors, they are polysemic terms. The set of possible interpretations is a set of institutionalized renderings, not new creations of meaning that could not have been communicated using previous modes of expression.

Symbols in ritual are pregnant with meaning. As Fernandez (1977) points out, symbols, by condensing many meanings, have a "multivocality or polysemy which makes them highly volatile" (p. 126). It is through this polysemy that a member's attention is shifted from one interpretive schema to another. For instance, according to Flumo, the boys' scarification is both a sign of membership and a representation of the *ngamu*'s teeth marks made when it symbolically ate the initiates when they entered into the fence. The design of the scars on the necks, chests, and backs of the boys refers to the particular Poro group or bush community that they joined. The leaves brought to town by the *kwelebah* in the *kanokowai* ritual also have multiple interpretations. According to one theme, they refer to the leaves that hunters use to carve up dead game; according to another, which focuses on the red latex inside the stems, they refer to the initiates' blood and their resurrection in the bush community. These meanings are present simultaneously in the ritual performance. The ability to formulate one or another is a condition of membership and of one's speaking rights relative to others in the situation.

The distinction to be made here is between ritual symbols that communicate different but institutionalized meanings to various categories of members and symbols that, like the living metaphors Ricouer speaks of, create new meanings through their situated uses. For instance, when a Zo makes a new medicine that has analogical properties to some ailment or condition, the act is a living metaphor in Ricouer's sense. I once attended a divination ritual where the Zo, or *teli pe nuu* (sand cutter), told the petitioner that he would be able to get a better job by using a certain fetish medicine regularly. The Zo instructed that, to make the medicine work, the petitioner would first have to give a gift to someone important and then take it away. The negative feelings generated would then guarantee that the medicine owner would soon be able to find work and that the job could never be taken from him. The medicine preparation contained symbols that were analogically different from their previous meanings. Taking a gift away, which has the culturally defined meaning of abuse, became a power that was directed by the medicine owner to his benefit in a novel situation.

Fernandez (1977) characterizes ritual metaphors as having a deep or underlying base that is reached by a transformation of metaphors through a quality space. A ritual is "a series of organizing images or metaphors put into operation by a series of superordinate and subordinate ceremonial scenes. Each of these scenes plays its part in realizing the implications of the image-play. . . . Through such ceremonial scenes, men become the metaphor predicated upon them" (Fernandez, 1974:125). The Poro initiations can, according to this perspective, be understood as the initiates' (or inchoate pronouns in Fernandez's terminology) undergoing a series of transformations from one set of sign-images or metaphors to another.

The predication of sign-images characterizes both living and dead metaphors. The secondary meanings, which are extensions of the first, state an equivalence between terms taken from separate semantic domains (cf. Sapir, 1977). In the case of *rat*, several negative attributes of rodents are projected, or predicated, upon human subjects so that the term comes to refer to a person with despicable characteristics. Predications are done through metaphorical extension (e.g., genus for genus), synecdoche (e.g., genus for species or species for genus), or metonymy (e.g., cause for effect). The symbols used in the rituals makes use of each of these forms. The initiation bush community is metaphorically called "inside the devil's stomach." The scars incised on the boy's necks, chests, and backs synecdochically refer to the particular bush community where they are initiated and metaphorically to the "teeth marks" of *ngamu*. The concealed acts of the members are metonymically referred to as *ngamu* or devil. In each case, the predication is so much a part of the expression that the original image is not posited. A member does not really think of a female devil's womb when he hears "inside the devil's stomach" but rather, of the bush village; similarly, one does not envision a rodent in response to "rat" referring to the pad on a woman's head or someone one dislikes, even though one can logically reconconstruct the etymological history of the expression.

When Ricouer refers to metaphors as "living," he means they result in a perception or understanding that previously did not exist. Such metaphors are not found in dictionary definitions; they have a unique elocutionary force. Hence, Ricouer argues for a rhetorical theory to account for them. The distinction between the two forms of metaphor is exemplified in a ritual that was performed by several leaders of the Sande

in Sucromu sometime about halfway through the ritual process of initiation into the Poro. The women came into the *loi kalong*'s compound
carrying fish nets and buckets of water. They wore old *lappa*s, and several
had rubbed their bodies with mud from the stream in front of the fence of
the bush community where the initiates were sequestered. The women
entered town and danced together in front of the chief's dwelling. Afterward, several Zo women came in from the stream with their bodies
completely covered with mud. Several of them lifted their *lappa*s in
mockingly lewd gestures. As the women did these acts, they chanted,
"We cast our nets into the water but bring back nothing in return." When
they finished rubbing the mud on one another, they bowed before and
accepted tribute kola from the *loi kalong*. Afterward, the Zo women who
had the buckets of water threw them on several of the performers and any
close bystander. They then left the quarter, continuing their chanting,
and performed in some of the other quarters of town. When the Poro Zo
leadership later met, they formally accused the women who organized the
performance of having exposed some of the Poro secrets.

The various symbols used in the performance—the fishnets, chants,
lifting of *lappa*s, and throwing of water on the bystanders—were
polysemic metaphors. The ritual is normally performed by women who
have experienced a series of consecutive stillbirths. The order of ritual
acts—the sequential progression of symbols in the event—is prescribed.
Each act has a set of meanings that refers directly to that intepretation.
When the ritual was enacted in the context of the Poro initiations,
however, the interpretation became a creative, or "living," metaphor: a
new meaning was established. The analogue was to the initiates in the
bush community and their liminal status. The reference to deceased
stillborn children became a metaphorical extension for the initiates.
Thus, a polysemic metaphor was transformed into a living metaphor. Its
appearance has a force that did not exist in previous enactments of the
ritual. This was taken to be a violation of the secrecy proscription that
pertains to all references by women to the reality of the initiation process.

In both the instances, the Zo's creative use of a cultural convention
about taking back gifts once given and the women in the fishnet ritual, the
respective metaphors led to understandings that previously did not exist.
Searle (1979), in his treatment of figurative language and indirect expression, has shown that, when one hears any speech act that is patently
incorrect or out of place, one immediately looks for a metaphoric usage.
Likewise, when the Poro Zo determined that the women's ritual was an
aberration, they immediately considered it to be a metaphoric extension
different from its normal metaphoric reference. Because they were not in
control of the use of the ritual metaphors, they deemed the performance
to be in violation of the Poro secrets.

The distinction between living and dead metaphors (or true metaphor and polysemy) does not account for how new members acquire knowledge through metaphors that are dead to the already initiated but quite alive for them. When the initiates are taken into the fence every Monday over the year-long ritual period, they formally learn that *ngamu* is not really a creature from the bush but is instead a theatrically performed illusion of the membership. That first encounter with the demasked *ngamu* has the rhetorical force of any living, or creative, metaphor. From then on, the new member learns to use the category *ngamu* as a polysemic expression whose varying meanings are occasioned by the situations in which the term is used.

Flumo used both discursive statements and metaphorical descriptions to refer to the same ritual events. For example, in response to my questions about the naming ritual at the end of the ritual process, he asserted,

> When they call their names at that time, they will say the devil will deliver.

He then immediately incorporated the pregnancy metaphor as a general gloss for the naming activity:

> And while the devil delivers, now they will start calling the names out.

Likewise, he substituted metaphorical glosses for direct descriptions in his discussion of the ritual of scarification. After he established that the scarring

> shows that everybody that you are a member,

he then used the devil gloss:

> That is the mark of the devil. Whenever the devil eating you like that, you see the devil eat you.

He continued to apply the "eating" metaphor in his later descriptions of the scarification ritual. He referred to the location where the ritual was performed as

> the camp is just like here, and the devil eats them.

Then, in response to how punishment is given during the ritual, he switched freely from an account of the act being done by a man to the devil-eating metaphor:

> When the devil was ready to eat him, the man who went there he was—sometimes they act bad, the man would start easy,

slowly, you know, the pain; the pain will hurt the person too much. And sometimes when the sun is hot, that is the time they do such. The devil start eating slowly, slowly.

Flumo also used metaphors to relate ritual acts to one another across the chain of ritual events. While the initiates undergo scarification (being eaten by the devil), the *kwelebah* announces the boys' death in the *juanay* ritual. After the boys enter the encampment where the other initiates reside, the men who accompanied them into the fence bring leaves into town in the *kanokowai* ritual. According to Flumo the *juanay* ritual "shows that the devil has killed the person," while the *kanokowai* ritual "means that the Zo has reborn you, the Zo have reborn me." Later, in his discussion of the rebirth during the naming ritual, Flumo associated the initiates' delivery with the devil rather than the Zo:

And the devil will go back, and it will stay long. It will call and it will deliver. So the devil born.

The statements that the Zo bring about rebirth during the *kanokowai* and the devil brings about during the naming ritual are not contradictory because they metaphorically refer to different states of being alive: in the forest and in the town, respectively. The initiates were symbolically killed and eaten as announced in the *juanay* ritual and reborn as announced during *kanokowai*. The former refers to the initiates' scarification, and the latter to their entrance into the initiation village. The devil kills, and the Zo give rebirth. The naming ritual, on the other hand, unites the entire chain of ritual events that occurred up to that point in the year-long ritual process. The initiates are taken into the forest, where they are killed and eaten by *ngamu*, they live in its stomach, and then they are reborn with new identities and names. It is the devil, not the Zo, who brings the boys back to the living community.

The term *ngamu* is a general gloss for activities done by the Poro membership in the various devils' names. It is a corporate category in the Weberian sense (Weber, 1947). Even the bringing of gifts into the initiation village to give to some relative is referred to as "carrying it to the devil." The terms *Zo* and *devil*, on the other hand, are quite distinct. It is the members of the Zo hierarchy that control the devils. They alone have the power to call them into town, have them make announcements to the community on behalf of the society, conduct sacrifices, be present during the adjudication of major disputes, and represent the society in relations with the other Poro organizations in different communities. Each of the Zo in the hierarchy is ranked according to the functions he performs in the society, whereas those who perform as the devils or do acts in their names are not so ranked. This is evident in Flumo's response to my question asking for the name of the person that performed the scarification operation:

FLUMO: A certain name? No, even a man like Gotojui can do it. Folpahzoi can do it.
BLB: So, you don't call them by a particular name?
FLUMO: No, no they don't call them that. They just call them *ngamu*. They are the devil.

Devil is thus a member-recognized metaphor for all activities done by the general membership. The type of activities included in that gloss are not confused with the *ngamu* masquerade performers. The metaphorical use of *ngamu* is a method for referring to all non-Zo activities that are done under the authority of the Zo leadership within Poro *meni*. The membership is controlled by the Zo in the same manner as is the *ngamu* masquerade performer. The relationship is metonymic in that it replaces contiguous terms that occupy a distinct and separate place within a single semantic domain. Here *act* is substituted for *agent*.

When Flumo distinguished between the medicines of the Poro and those of the Zo, he made use of this metonymic substitution. He asserted that the only medicine that is associated directly with the Poro is *ngamu*. The knowledge and ability to act on its behalf is the real power of the society. The Zo, on the other hand, have their own medicines. The Poro provides the relevant *meni* as a meaning context for them to put their respective medicines together for the general benefit of the larger community. To be a member of Poro does not make one privy to those medicines. The children of the Zo must learn them from their fathers independent of the instruction that the other members receive when they enter the society.

Although they interact with the other initiates in most activities inside the initiation community, the children of the Zo undertake their different instruction, make separate sacrifices, and when any poultry is served, eat separately. Poultry is associated with sacrifice. All objects of sacrifice, whether they be goats, cows, or chickens, are always referred to as *tee*, literally 'chicken.' Even in the illegal societies that practice human sacrifice, the person killed is referred to as a chicken. Thus, the Zo always distinguish themselves from the membership. This is expressed formally in the relation between the Zo and the different types of *noi sheng* or *ngamu*. When the *ngamu* are performed, they represent the power of the Zo, who are always in control of their movements. Likewise, when *ngamu* is used as a metaphor for the general membership of the society, the Zo also control their behavior. Hence, the Zo hierarchy is over *ngamu* in each of its symbolic forms.

Power relations among Zo, devil, members, and nonmembers are continually expressed in the forms of ritual discourse used during the various stages of the initiation process. In the following chapter, I attend to the types of formal oratory in order to examine the methods employed for communicating concealed information within ritual acts.

7
Mentioning
the Unmentionable

The distinction between rituals of illusion and allusion is part of the sociology of knowledge that defines categories of members and distinguishes them from the different categories of nonmembers. The former refers to grades of membership within the Poro and its internal associations, as well as to membership in the various supportive secret societies (the Mina and Moling) and medicine associations (Kale Sale, Kawli Sale, Gbo Sale, etc.). The categories of nonmembers include the women of the Sande, uninitiated young men and boys who plan to enter the Poro during the ritual process, and Mandingo who choose not to join. Upon becoming a member of the Poro, one learns that various manifestations are theatrically produced illusions. From then on, all one's references to the illusions are metaphorical and therefore allusions. In cases where the knowledge that some manifestation is an illusion is shared by nonmembers, initiation involves the acquisition of the right to profess the knowledge rather than to be constrained and always having to use forms of indirect reference.

The Operation and Transformation of Metaphors in Ritual

The characterization of ritual as the transformation of metaphors within an image-play such that participants become the metaphors predicated upon them is particularly relevant to the Poro initiation process. The first ritual act is the capture of the initiates by the *kwelebah*, whence they are forced to recognize referents for the ritual metaphors that will become transformed during the stages of the ritual process. The initiates must formally assert that the *ngamu* is a creature in the forest with which they are to do battle. They are required to affirm the existence of the ritual metaphors by taking part in the dramatic play that they are warrior-hunters who will not only fight and kill the devil but bring back portions of it for the townspeople to eat. If a boy is hesitant in affirming the metaphor, the members persist in chiding him until he does.

The following translated dialogue is from a video recording made of the entry into the bush of two boys from the Zo family who joined near the beginning of the initiation period. Both were terrified not only of the painful ritual acts to come but at the prospect of remaining for a full year in the bush village. The boys were selected as among the first because neither was attending school that year. Although most youth express a desire to go to school, in fact less than 15 percent are able to do so. Gwiimeni claimed, nevertheless, that he wanted to enter school that year and ran to the market town of Zorzor to escape the *kwelebah*. Several men in his family followed him there and forcibly brought him back. The dialogue begins as he is sitting on the bench in front of the house of the Zo to whom initiates are brought after the thatch sash is tied on them. He is surrounded by the men in his family while they wait for Bobo, the second boy, to arrive.

KORKULAH: Gwiimeni is standing ahead tomorrow. Who will I ask?

MULBAH: No one has asked me yet.

KORKULAH: That kind of matter is easy to understand.

GWIIMENI: I don't want to be involved.

KORKULAH: He won't drink some cane juice from Palapulu [the farming village of the boy's family] now.

FOLPAHZOI: You wait and see Bobo [the other boy] dance here. This one is too afraid.

KORKULAH: You are the one to slap it; we will be behind you.

SUMO: I will give you a knife [the wooden sword].

FLUMO: Wait, let me go for the food so that you will eat and go to bed.

FOLPAHZOI: Bring the players [musicians] to play for this child.

ZUAZEN: This is the sword; bring the head if you kill it.

FOLPAHZOI: You are going to make yourself shamed.

KORKULAH: This is the answer. He is not sleeping here. He and I are going to the bush.

FOLPAHZOI: Wait until Bobo comes. They are two.

PEWU: If this one sleeps here, he will run away.

GWIIMENI: Where will I go if I run away?

SUMO: Cannot you be very satisfied and play [i.e., dance with the musicians and fellow members]?

KORKULAH: You should give him a knife to struggle [dance] with.

PEWU: Wait to see Bobo dance [*kawngaw*, which literally means 'to struggle'] before you when he comes.

FLUMO: That kind of person, if he had been a different person, he would laugh at him [If you were looking at someone else you would be laughing at him].

KORKULAH: If you cannot kill it in the night, will you kill it tomorrow morning?

PEWU: If this one sleeps here, we will look for him.

FOLPAHZOI: If he is afraid, Bobo will remain here and dance.

ZUAZEN: We who are all around you, we put a knife in your hand and you say no.

FLUMO: Who went to bring Bobo?

PEWU: Bobo had cried and they took him from town. I caught him under my orange tree and he said he took from under it.

FLUMO: They are the ones that are damaging my sugar cane.

FOLPAHZOI: Didn't you come to me before and tell me that you would kill the devil and now you cry?

KORKULAH: They gave his knife and he said that he cannot hold it.

FLUMO: Everyone should open the door.

(Bobo enters the area and the men begin to dance with the two boys around the community. They reach the part of the compound where the boys' *ngala* reside. Everyone dances in a circle with the boys. Folpahzoi blows his whistle to gain the attention of everyone. He then addresses Gwiimeni.)

FOLPAHZOI: You are supposed to calm your younger brother. You should tell him to bear patience. Let your heart be on me [trust me].

KORKULAH: This is a woman's rich child [a child raised by a mother and who is not brave].

PEWU: They have taken the abusing child from the quarter.

FOLPAHZOI: Everyone come and dress them.

FLUMO: You shouldn't scold the child.

KORKULAH: Tell him "I will kill the devil tomorrow."

FOLPAHZOI: You have the devil's cloth [the thatch sash] on your neck.

ZUAZEN: They are giving presentations to everyone.

PEWU: The owners have come now. Don't worry.

FLUMO: Women cannot do some of this play.

FOLPAHZOI: Call the owner of this thing [the boys].

MULBAH: There are many *meni* in life. He should get a bag of bread, that is hernia sickness. He should have clothes on the neck, that is reddish skin rash. He and thatch they should fight war, that is blindness sickness. That which remains is the new generation. The people are looking for involvement [*la meni*, literally, 'mouth matter'].

FOLPAHZOI: I have a warrior here. Bobo, if you kill it, which part will you give me? (after a moment's silence) You told me before that you are going to kill it. He said he will give me the head. Gwiimeni, you are the eldest person. If you kill it, which part will you give me?

(There are several people talking at once. Folpahzoi blows the whistle again to get their attention and continues to speak.)

FOLPAHZOI: You wait, I want to ask my people.

GWIIMENI: My hand cannot fit on it [he refuses to pledge to kill the devil].

FOLPAHZOI: I am asking Bobo again. Bobo, what did you say to me?

BOBO: I will give you the head.

(At that, everyone cheered and several handed Bobo coins as a tribute.)

FOLPAHZOI: Gwiimeni, your younger brother said he will give me the head. You are the eldest person, my mind is now on you. You have for a long time been killing animals. You know the sweetest part. What part will you give to satisfy me?

ZUAZEN: Give him that part of the animal that can satisfy an old man. Perhaps it is the *nlila* [the front of the abdomen, which is usually cooked and eaten in the bush by the hunters; women are forbidden from eating any].

GWIIMENI: I cannot kill the devil.

FOLPAHZOI: He said he is unable to kill the devil.

(Several people cheer at Gwiimeni's response and hand him coins.)

FOLPAHZOI: Before I do anything, is necessary to reach your place.

Afterward, the group moved into another section of the compound to receive the blessing of the quarter chief, Kaboku.

FOLPAHZOI: Kaboku, it reaches you. Here are the children.

KABOKU: The ones that are in town, the ones that are in the bush. All should have clear skin [good health].

EVERYONE: *Mayna* [a blessing response].

KABOKU: It should be as a cassava leaf bunch. May God make many possible.

EVERYONE: *Mayna.*

KABOKU: That which touches something and makes it spoil should not touch you.

EVERYONE: *Mayna.*

KABOKU: You go safely, you come safely. God make that possible.

EVERYONE: *Mayna.*

FOLPAHZOI: Bobo, you are the owner of the quarter. This is our ancestor. His name is on this quarter.

The group then performed in each of the other quarters in town.

Once the *japa*, or sash, is tied on the initiates' chests, the boys are transformed by the ritual metaphors predicated on them. They become characters in a kind of dramatic play in which they are forced to participate as actors. Wooden swords with their points either painted red or dipped in chicken blood are placed in their hands. Male relatives then tie head ties on their heads and attach other ties to their clothes to give them something to wear in battle. This also establishes the initiates' liminal status. They are no longer children and not yet men; so they wear the head ties of women. As characters in the play, they cooperate by accepting these symbols and their part as warrior-hunters. Although the quoted dialogue concerned boys who were reluctant, others accept their parts much more easily. As the initiates dance, they are told to lift their wooden swords in a portrayal of warriors. Hence, the dance is referred to as a "struggle" (*kawngaw*) rather than a "play" (*pili*). If a boy should lower or drop his arm, the members immediately raise it and give a harsh warning. The boys are constantly watched; even when a boy needs to urinate during the dance in town, he must ask permission and then is accompanied by a member to insure not only that he not escape but that no women come near. The members all joke among each other but are very stern with the boys. This strict attitude continues throughout the entire ritual process until they are presented to the *loi kalong* at the end.

The boys are made aware of the various themes in the ritual process through their active participation in the dramatic play. They are told they must fight the devil, and they know that no one could win such a battle. The blessings they receive all foretell their eventual resurrection after metaphorical death. When the boys enter into the Poro fence, they carry their innocence as well as the evils the community wants to be rid of. The boys are teased for their bad behavior.

> I caught him under my orange tree and he said he took from under it.
>
> They are the ones that are damaging my sugar cane.

> This is a woman's rich child [a spoiled child].
> They have taken the abusing child from the quarter.

All of a boy's delinquent acts are forgotten when he is symbolically killed. In the last chapter, the case of Nuita was mentioned during the course of my discussion with Flumo. Nuita had consistently gotten into trouble and had often been caught stealing. One afternoon he was caught eating a chicken, which he had carried into a vacant house and killed. His father asked the *kwelebah* to carry him to the Poro fence the next day. He was given an especially painful scarification and was under strict supervision in the bush community.

Blessings are given that contain a kind of curse. The presenter prays that the initiates will catch illnesses and misfortunes to take into the bush with them. There, by undergoing metaphorical death, the boys eliminate evils from the community. In the translated dialogue, Mulbah gave such a blessing:

> There are many *meni* in life. He should get a bag of bread, that is hernia sickness. He should have clothes on the neck, that is reddish skin rash. He and thatch they should fight war, that is blindness sickness. That which remains is the new generation. The people are looking for involvement.

These conditions are considered to be both incurable and the result of violations of laws of medicines and lineage prohibitions. Hernias are believed to be the result of men having come too close to the medicines of the Sande society. To have a hernia means the patient violated Sande law and must do special penance to the society's Zo. A reddish skin rash is the result of having broken one's *tinya*, or family food taboo. Blindness is incurable and often the result of witchcraft. Hence, Mulbah's blessing had different levels of meaning. It referred both to the expulsion of evil from the town through the vehicle of the boy's metaphorical death and to a delineation of maladies caused by human agencies: Sande; family; and *sale nyomo*, or bad medicines.

Metaphor Transformations in the Concluding Part of the Initiation Rituals

The ritual process continues throughout each of its stages as a kind of theatrical play. The following is an example of dialogues the *ngamu* had with the community leaders just before the closing of the bush almost a year after the first initiates entered. I present this data in full, both as an example of the kinds of blessings and discussions the *ngamu* has with the members and for its importance as the announcement that the rituals will end the next month.

After the initiates have danced in each of the quarters and their relatives have presented them with head ties, bottles of Fanta, and small change, the announcement is made that the devil is coming out. All nonmembers enter their houses. After a few minutes the devil leaves the fence and goes to the quarter of the eldest boy who will enter into the fence the following morning. The *ngamu* greets the father or sponsor of the initiate and is given some money as symbolic kola. The *kwelebah* translates the *ngamu*'s trill language. In the following transcript, speeches labeled *Ngamu* are actually the translations of the *kwelebah*, whereas speeches labeled *Kwelebah* are his own dialogue rather than *ngamu*'s.

NGAMU: Thank you for your donation. Some boys are going into the bush tomorrow. I am going now to look for another to join him. I am so old. If you go to a parent's farm and you eat a part of the animal that you are not supposed to eat, and you eat it, you may result in having a sore throat. Listen *Kwelebah*! I want to go to Malawu.

KWELEBAH: No, this is not the time.

NGAMU: Then why are they behaving like that? You should bear patience until the time reaches (the *kwelebah* says this in a loud voice to insure that those inside hear).

KORKULAH: I have a boy who is ready to go.

NGAMU: Where is he?

BUKOLUAH: The devil's wife cannot get tired; she can kill as many humans as is possible.

NGAMU: Thank you for what you have said. I want to know where is the boy you promised me.

(The musicians play for several minutes until the *ngamu* stops them. The *ngamu* speaks through the *kwelebah* interpreter to Nyamasimaka, a Zo from Guinea who accompanied a group of initiates coming to Sucromu to join the Poro.)

NGAMU: Thank you for all you have done. Whenever I come to town, I must visit certain people here because they are very important. If I do not visit them, they might fail with him. I am grateful for what you are trying to do for the society. What little money that you have left after giving, may that little amount now increase. May it increase enough that you are able to add to your household in general. I am now going to give this money to the Zo. It is not for me. Although I am thankful, I will be more thankful for the *sina* [the nonmember] because the money is for the Zo and not for me.

(Several background noises interrupt the *ngamu*.)

NGAMU: *Kwelebah*, be quiet. If you are so drunk you should go to bed to avoid trouble.

NGAMU: Every human being has the same attitude. There is a God, there is no food right now, there is no money, there is no bitter-ball. May you have all of these things in abundance at a later time to come. I am very old. My wife is very old. But we are not too old for mankind, the Poro society. For the respect that Nyamasimaka has been paying to the Poro and Sande societies that they should always have blessing and play this major role in society forever and ever. That way it will always be very great. Those boys that went into the bush and even those still in town that respect the Zo business, I give you a very good blessing. You should be successful in life. Those that do not pay any attention to Zo business, I give you the bad blessing [curse]. They should never be successful in whatever they undertake to do. In case the person should go to a Zo for a medicine or even a *kwii* doctor [Western medical doctor], the person should never be healthful. The person should never be helpful in case of curing the person. I want a *sina* now. Why, *Kwelebah*, do you bring this kind of attitude toward me?

KWELEBAH: It is just Monday and I am trying to hear what you are saying toward your request.

(Musicians play again. The *ngamu* shouts above the music.)

NGAMU: Bring me a trouble person so that I can get some money.

(The procession goes into the compound of Vallai, the *loi kalong*. They stop before Vallai's house.)

NGAMU: Chief Vallai, I greet you. Business is business [*meni kaa meni*].

KWELEBAH: I could tell the good news, but it is hard to talk to the devil. However, I wish the Poro good. The thing which goes on should be extended for two years, rather than just one year. This is good for Chief Vallai to hear because he makes all the important decisions in the town. He is the right person to hear about such a situation.

NGAMU: I heard something and I want to find out if it is true. I was in the bush and a breeze blew in my ear, but I have not found the truth yet.

FLUMO [Chief Vallai's eldest son, who during the initiations assumed his father's position as the landlord]: What is the news here?

NGAMU: The news is that I heard from Bakolleah, the old man in Zoman quarter, that they are closing the bush tomorrow. No other person should go in there again. I want to know if this news is true.

FLUMO: I speak in behalf of my father, and I do not know if this news is true. But maybe my father knows it. As far as I am concerned, we still have eleven more months to go with the *kuu* [initiations].

NGAMU: If you walk on the green slime, it is so slippery that if you do not hold your toes in the ground, you might slip and fall. So, Flumo says that there are ten months remaining and just one day. I do not agree. There is much left for me to take care of business. Flumo says that the time to end friendship is tomorrow. Flumo should bring thirty more boys to join the others tomorrow. The business should be done that way it should be done. You should do good for someone who will appreciate it. When I go around town, I hear everyone saying that pretty soon the ugly devil will go out of town.

KWELEBAH: Once the devil insisted that they close down the schools so the boys can go into the bush. I want to know if my own can be closed.

NGAMU: You are in the same mood as Flumo to have the bush terminated tomorrow.

KWELEBAH: No, I am loyal; I cannot do that to the *ngamu*.

FLUMO: *Kwelebah*, tell the devil that the good friendship that exists between us. I am the only one who can give something to the friend and the friend never give something in return. So, because I am not getting anything from the friend to eat, I am going to draw back and just sit down and we will just sit and look at one another.

NGAMU: I want you to bring one hundred more boys to join the others and then I will give something in return for that. As human beings when the man goes in the bush in the morning and comes back in the evening, if he has something in the bag for the wife, he will first wait until the wife takes the bag from his shoulder. He will wait for whatever the wife has for him. If she cooks some rice for him and kept it for him, then after eating he will put his hand in his bag and take out some object and present it to the woman for return.

(The musicians begin to play. After a few minutes the devil gives some blessings to Flumo.)

NGAMU: Thank you for your kindness. I want us to renew our friendship. We should have a better friendship this time.

(The musicians accompany the procession to another quarter. As they dance the musicians play a special song—"Zo business is like darkness and the Zo bush is far out of town." The *ngamu* goes to the house of Labulah and greets him. Labulah gives some money to him, and the devil gives Labulah a blessing.)

NGAMU: I will take this money to the Zo, to Mulbah Jackollie in town. For the respect that you have paid to me you should be very successful in whatever you attempt to do. The little money that you have left, you should prosper. There are things that if a man undertakes other men will respect him in turn and that you always enjoy Poro and Sande business on this earth. There is one thing that you Labulah have that you will never give to anybody. No matter how you love a woman or no matter how you become friendly with a man that you will not give to the person. That is life. You should live as long as time cannot shave our heads [make us bald from old age]. Labulah, you should have the kind of good fortune that a cassava stick has. That is, you should cut a piece and throw it somewhere in the bush, it will still grow. That wherever you go you may prosper. That you should lead a good life and be successful in whatever you try to do.

(The musicians begin to play. The *ngamu* gives a warning that those who are drunk should go to bed to avoid trouble.)

NGAMU: (To the *kwelebah*) Have you ever seen the devil fall outside?
KWELEBAH: No. But other people are getting drunk and might tend to fall.
NGAMU: I have some boys to kill tomorrow and I will fight. I am sure that I will be victorious. I will grind them and put them in my wife's stomach. I owe the devil in Kpaiyea some *sina*s and I don't have enough to pay the devil in Kpaiyea back. I need more boys so that I can pay my debt and have more for my wife.
KWELEBAH: Many people are getting drunk. The best way to look for trouble is to slap the wife of Jackollie [the head Zo of the hierarchy], or to beat some of the Zo, that is the person that goes look for trouble.
NGAMU: I don't know how a case like that could be settled unless the

person would have to die to pay. I want to hear another song now, sing "*Menikaw kaa*" ("A Mandingo man cannot see it").

(Langba, a visitor from Guinea, gives some money to *ngamu* and greets him.)

NGAMU: I wish you good fortune. May you return home safely. May you never have hard luck such as your brother dies and his wife comes to stay with you. Since you are a traveler, whatever car you ride, it should go safely. In case you go in the bush, you should never meet a hunter.

(The *ngamu* then turns to Tokpah, who was assigned the duties of a Zo who died a few years ago.)

NGAMU: You are yourself a *ngamu*, the *ngamu* of the man.
TOKPAH: I want the musicians to sing "If a Zo born, his son is not just a Zo."

(The musicians sing his request.)

KWELEBAH: I want now to hear the song "A learning Zo does not know the right leaves" and "A frisky woman does not know how responsible her husband is."

(The musicians sing the request.)

MULBAH: *Ngamu*, all the schools in town are now closed in town.
NGAMU: Then you should release all of the boys so that they can go into the bush.
SUMO [One of the Zo]: I want us now to go into the fence.
KWELEBAH: One of the Zo has requested we go now to the fence.
NGAMU: I will go into the fence because I am owned by the Zo and the Zo have greater power than I do.

(The musicians play as the procession moves toward the fence. The song played is always the last that is played before the *ngamu* retires from a performance. On the way, One Day, an elder from Zokolomii quarter, approaches the *ngamu* and gives him some money on behalf of one of the Sande Zo women, Cortoe.)

NGAMU: Tell Cortoe that I thank her for being kind and for being so nice to the Zo whenever I come into town. It is wise to tell a nice person that he is nice than to tell a rogue that you are always a rogue. That woman is an example of a nice person, she is always nice to the Zo whenever the devil comes to town.

(The *ngamu* then tells everyone to behave and that if anyone is drunk that he should go to bed.)

NGAMU: Even if you be nice to me, if you are drunk and cause trouble, you will still have to pay fine.

BAKOLLEAH: *Kwelebah*, please share the cane juice with us that you have.

KWELEBAH: Yes, let us take the log.

NGAMU: The school will be closed soon. But for my own it cannot be closed. Because if they drive me from Sucromu, I can still go to Malawu.

(The procession then goes inside the fence.)

The *ngamu* performed as a character in a theatrical play in his visits to the quarters. He came to town for the express purpose of announcing that the initiation rituals were about to close, and he made the announcement in the compound of the *loi kalong*, Waiquai Vallai, through the use of a coded dialogue with Vallai's son, Flumo. As the *ngamu* entered town, he announced that he was looking for a *sina* to take into the bush with him. He then used a parable about having to be cautious when eating, to inform the listeners about the necessity of being discriminating when accepting initiates. Because the ritual was performed near the end of the ritual period, the *ngamu*'s statement meant that he did not want to accept any boys that would cause trouble in the bush community. At that, he announced his desire to go to the Loma community of Malawu, whose bush would close after that of Sucromu. The assertion served notice that those who do not join the Sucromu Poro in the next few weeks would have to go to Malawu for initiation. The *kwelebah*'s negative reply announced that the time for the ending of Sucromu's initiation was close but had not yet come.

The *ngamu*'s question, "Why are they behaving like that?," referred to the community's preparation for the forthcoming celebrations when the boys would leave the fence. Groups of tailors were busy sewing country cloth gowns and hats for the initiates to wear when they enter Sucromu. The *ngamu*'s assertion that the people should "bear patience" was loudly proclaimed by his *kwelebah* translator.

Kokulah, the father of the eldest initiate who was going to enter when the boys were next carried into the fence, then approached the *ngamu* and announced that his son was ready to go. One of the Zo, Bukoluah, said that the *ngamu*'s wife can kill as many humans as possible. This represents a shift in metaphoric imagery from the *ngamu* as the killer of initiates, to his wife. As this performance occurred near the end of the ritual process, the idea expressed was that the *ngamunea* had taken many children into her womb. During the first part of the ritual process, the *ngamu*'s wife was not directly mentioned, as the initiates were said to be "killed by *ngamu*" and "reborn by the Zo" in the "stomach of the *ngamu*." Now that the ritual process is near its end, the stomach of the *ngamu* becomes transformed into the womb of his wife. Hence, it is the wife who can "kill as many humans as possible." The *ngamu* responded to Kokulah that he would accept his son and rhetorically asked for the boy. At that, the musicians played for several minutes, until they were stopped by the *ngamu*. During their performance the Zo leader of the Guineans presented the *ngamu* with a money token. The *ngamu* thanked him and announced that the money was not for him, but instead for the Zo. In so doing, the *ngamu* communicated his position relative to the Zo hierarchy: they control him, permit his presence, and use his powers for the general protection of the community.

Ngamu praised Nyamasimaka, an important elder in the quarter, and in his name both blessed the boys who joined the society and those who planned to enter and cursed those disrespectful to the Zo. After the blessing, the *ngamu* asked again for a *sina*, and the *kwelebah* responded that it was only Monday (the initiates were taken into the bush each Monday). The interchange, which was a repetition of the *ngamu*'s earlier request, was performed as a transition ritual act leading to the next order of business: the announcement to be made to the *loi kalong*.

As the *ngamu* walked toward the *loi kalong*'s quarter, he asked for any troublemaker to come so that he could exact a fine. In so doing, he established the solemnity of the interaction to follow. The procession came before Vallai's house. *Ngamu* greeted him. What followed was a highly coded dialogue between the *ngamu*; the *kwelebah*; Vallai; and Flumo, Vallai's eldest son, who in the course of the initiations took over his father's position as the owner of the land.

The *kwelebah* spoke of the success of the initiation and stated to Vallai that the initiations should really go on for two years instead of one. The *ngamu* said that he had heard gossip that troubled him and wanted to find out the truth. At that, Flumo asked his question-salutation *Ku meni naa?* and in so doing established his position as *loi kalong* in place of his father. The *ngamu* then spoke directly to him, saying that he heard from the Zo *nang*, Bakolleah Gbonopili, that the bush was going to close the next day. As the Zo *nang*, Bakolleah was the spokesman for all the Zo. Flumo answered, "As far as I am concerned, we still have eleven more months to go with the *kuu*." In Kpelle, the term for "eleven" is *puu kau tano* ("ten plus one"). The *ngamu* recognized that Flumo was speaking in code by proffering the parable "If you walk on the green slime, it is so slippery that if you do not hold your toes in the ground, you might slip and fall." The green slime is an allusion to the slippery growths on rocks in swampy areas of the bush. The *ngamu* then repeated what Flumo said but changed the wording, saying that Flumo claimed there were ten months and *one day* remaining. By changing *puu kau tano* to *puu nalong e xele tano* ("ten months and one day"), the *ngamu* asserted that Flumo really meant that the boys should come out the following day. The *ngamu* then asked the *kwelebah* if he agreed. The *kwelebah* said that he was loyal to the *ngamu*. This was significant because the *kwelebah* is a member of the secular part of the community and, as the nephew of the Zo, serves both them and the devil. In his statement of loyalty, he symbolically reaffirmed the community's commitment to the Poro.

Flumo then debated with the *ngamu* through the *kwelebah*, complaining that the community had given many youth but had received nothing in return (viz., indirectly requesting that the initiates be brought back into the community). In so doing, he questioned the friendship between the Poro and the community. The *ngamu* answered by demanding one hundred more initiates and then presented the parable about how a man will wait until his wife takes his bag from his shoulder and offers him what she has before putting his hand in the bag and giving what he has brought to her. Thus, the *ngamu* announced that the initiations would continue for a while longer. The musicians then played, followed by the *ngamu*'s blessings to Flumo, which reestablished their friendship and, thereby, the alliance between the sacred and the secular political structures of the community.

As the *ngamu* procession left the quarter, the musicians played a special song, which was a call for all nonmembers to join. According to my assistants, the song "Zo business is like darkness and the Zo bush is far out of town" means:

> It is like darkness. If you are not in the darkness, you don't
> know what is happening there. And the only way that you
> can know what is in the darkness is to go out and see what
> is happening there.

The remainder of the *ngamu*'s walk involved his greeting various important personages and receiving tribute in return for his gnomic blessings. On the way to the area where the leader of the Guineans resided, the *ngamu* requested a song sung in Loma: "*Menikaw kaa*," meaning "A Mandingo man cannot see it." As Mandingos will not join the Poro, the song exhibited the special status that the Guineans will have by being Poro members in the country controlled by a Mandingo government. When the *ngamu* had greeted the Guinean leader, he turned to the Guineans' new head Zo, Tokpah, who had come to Sucromu for additional training. This Zo had only recently taken power, after the death of his father. The *ngamu* greeted him by saying, "You are yourself a *ngamu*, the *ngamu* of the man," thus using the concept of devil metaphorically to refer to the continuation of the deceased Zo's spirit through the body of his successor.

Tokpah responded by requesting a song "If a Zo born, his son is not just a Zo," which praised his father's powers. The *kwelebah* answered with the dual request "A learning Zo does not know the right leaves" and "A frisky woman does not know how responsible her husband is." The three songs point to Tokpah's apprenticeship status as a Zo. He had come from Guinea for his instruction in Poro rituals. The Zo's song recognized his position under the Sucromu Zo, and the *kwelebah*'s request underlined the importance of his instruction.

Mulbah, the principal of the government school, then informed the *ngamu* that the school was closed for the students to join the society. The *ngamu* responded by asking for the boys. Then, one of the Zo requested that the *ngamu* return to the Zo fence. The *ngamu*'s reply again established the position of the devil relative to the Zo: "I will go into the fence because I am owned by the Zo and the Zo have greater power than I do." As the *ngamu* went into the fence, he declared that the bush would soon be closed but that it would continue in Malawu. This was a repetition of his statement made at the beginning of his walk and again served notice that those who do not join in Sucromu must go to Malawu.

The interactions the *ngamu* had with Flumo and his father, Vallai, were determined before the devil came to town. The Zo in concert with the secular ruling structure (the landlord, chiefs, and elders) had already set the date for the ending of the initiation rituals. The date of closing coordinated with the ending of the bush in each of the other Kpelle communities in the chiefdom, and it preceded the closing of the bush in Malawu, the home of the *da* Zo (head government Zo). The dates were given to the Ministry of Local Goverment in Monrovia for final approval before the opening of the Poro bush. Thus, the debate between the *ngamu* and Flumo was a dramatic presentation scripted according to the overall theatrical play about the initiates being killed, ground up in the devil's mouth, put into the wife's stomach, and reborn.

Symbols of Transformation

The conclusion of the dramatic play is the ritual of rebirth when the initiates are given their new Poro names. Although the names are previously given to them in the bush community (as the interview with Flumo in the previous chapter showed), in the rebirth ritual the initiates formally take the names and their concomitant status as Poro members.

In the afternoon of the ritual, the *ngamu* makes a public appearance in the community. He appears without any previous warning from the bush. This time, when he arrives, there is no call for the nonmembers to enter into their houses. The *ngamu* enters town and immediately goes into the Zo fence. A short time later, he visits every quarter and proclaims that his wife is in labor and will soon give birth. He makes special visits to the house of the family of the *Folpah* (the initiate who was first to enter into the bush fence and who will be first to reenter town after the rebirth ritual) and to the *tipinenu* (the woman member of Poro), with whom he dances for several minutes before finally leaving for the initiation village.

That evening the *kwelebah* announces that all doors are to be closed. Then the *ngamu* enters town and walks through each of the quarters on his way to Vallai's house. There he stops and calls aloud:

NGAMU: Tell him that I am walking about. Tell Vallai that he has received a stranger. Unless I greet Vallai when I come here, it is not good. The *loi kalong* owns the Zo and the Zo owns the devil. The devil cannot control the Zo.

VALLAI: I greet you with this kola.

NGAMU: There are many medicines in the mortar. Whatsoever the Zo presents to me, it is good for the Zo. It is for them in any case. The thing that can kill a person's child, mine is not going. A person that chases from one frog to another can cause a person to remain in frog water.

VALLAI: That is good.

NGAMU: (To those who are surrounding him) Poro members [*kwiyɓela*] the hook dropped by me is carefulness. An amateur Zo does not know leaves. The *ngamu*'s pregnancy [a dangerous period] is on you [current in the community]; keep away from it.

(The procession then goes to visit the other quarters in town. As they walk, the *ngamu* engages in a discussion with the head singer, or *yabolo*.)

YABOLO: If the devil likes a person, then he has lost respect. If you are doing witch [*wulu*], have its body in your hand. A person should not do it in the human [*nuula*—also a form for family] way. The Zo says *kokoi* [success]. Give the song to the singer; he is the one that knows how to sing it. If you are good to me in the *kuu*, I will be good to you.

NGAMU: A snake cannot dig its own hole. Being in Monrovia is big news. If you and someone become friends, don't let the person's wife be leopard's food. If you take a large snail, you have taken all into one [all matters are being taken care of at one time]. Tomorrow is another daybreak. Let us think ahead for tomorrow. This matter has existed for a long time. Poro members, these words are right?

KWELEBAH: The Zo said they are satisfied.

NGAMU: Thank him over two or three times. What is it that is laid on me? The matter is a sorrowful *meni*.

YABOLO: They are afraid of death. Mine did not wash the traveling clothes. If you travel in the night, you will see what is inside.

NGAMU: Show me the road. I talk to you; you talk to him.

YABOLO: Mine is in the hands of a learning Zo. They tied me until they carried my child away.

NGAMU: Kindness says praise, that is, if you do it, the person will know it. There is still some remaining in the back of my hand. Come trouble seeker!

KWELEBAH: It is still outside.

YABOLO: You remain after love until your clothes burn [you keep after a lover until you get hurt].

NGAMU: Extend your words to Welikaw's son [i.e., Vallai's son, Flumo]. There are only eleven months. I cannot see any defender now. If you eat your taboo, the matter [*meni*] will remain on you. He [the *ngamu*] is behind me to take my person from me [i.e., his is not paying respect].

YAKPAWOLO: We will do some behind the thick bush tomorrow.

NGAMU: (Directly to the *kwelebah*) The coming out night says morning. Spying cannot see it unless you look on it.

KWELEBAH: Twins [The Poro and the Sande] cannot be in the sun's stomach.

NGAMU: Your child that you gave to me, his name is Caterpillar. Listen to me!

KWELEBAH: (Speaking for Yakpawolo) He says that he cannot accept that.

(The procession then goes to a fence just outside of Sucromu that is adjacent to the Moling society bush. There, the initiates stand in a long line facing in the direction of the washing fence about a quarter of a mile away. Several of the elders ask that the *ngamu* personally name their sons in the ritual, and in so asking, they make a presentation of money to the Zo. The *ngamu* then begins.)

FLUMO: I want to request of *Ngamu* that he names my son.

NGAMU: The name of your son is Worm.

FLUMO: I cannot accept it.

NGAMU: His name is Frog.

FLUMO: I cannot accept that either.

NGAMU: His name is Insect.

FLUMO: I don't accept it.

NGAMU: His name is Caterpillar.
FLUMO: I cannot accept it.
NGAMU: His name is Bokulo.
FLUMO: I do not accept it.
NGAMU: Listen good, *Kwelebah*! I am going to rename Flumo's son.
His name is Folpah.

(At that, all in attendance give a resounding cheer.)

NGAMU: I am now going to name Kwaywu's son. His name is Frog.
KWAYWU: I refuse it.
NGAMU: His name is Caterpillar.
KWAYWU: I cannot accept it.
NGAMU: All right, I bring it again. His name is Worm.
KWAYWU: I refuse it.
KWELEBAH: Worm, Worm, Worm, Worm, Worm, Worm.
KWAYWU: No, I don't accept it.
NGAMU: His name is Bokulo.
KWAYWU: I still refuse it.
NGAMU: His same is Sumowolo Kwelebah.

(Again, everyone cheers loudly.)

The *ngamu* goes on to name the boys of several of the elders and Zo in the hierarchy. The only boy he names directly is the son of the *kwelebah*, Yakpazua Kennai. After announcing the latter's name, the *ngamu* tells everyone to go to his own house and those of his family to tell the occupants the names of their children and those in their care. The men then go to their houses, where their women wait impatiently inside. As they tell the women the names of the boys, the women cheer loudly. A short time later, the *ngamu* goes into the fence. The initiates are then led to the washing bush, where they spend the night. After all the initiates are inside the fence, the town opens up and everyone celebrates with dancing and drinking until daybreak.

The next morning, women carry hot water and food to the front of the fence. There, the members carry the goods inside. The initiates bathe, eat, and put on gowns specially prepared for their entry into the community. Hats, which are decoratively covered with dozens of safety pins, are placed on their heads and fitted over their eyebrows.

In the late afternoon, just before sundown, the *kwelebah* runs through the town, ringing his bell. The young women who joined the Sande during the last initiation period all leave town. (I was told that previously they would have spent the night on their farms, but on this occasion they are merely required to leave for the entry of the boys. Many, nevertheless, carry bundles of clothes on their heads as if prepared to stay away for the night.) A short time after the women leave, the announcement is made for the doors to be shut as if the *ngamu* were going to appear. During this period, the boys are led from the washing bush to the area just outside of town where, the evening before, they had undergone the rebirth ritual.

The boys are positioned first by *taa* (Sucronsu or Twasamu) and then by their respective *kolii*. As they form their lines, elders shout their orders to them and hit them with switches if they respond too slowly. The *kwelebah* then leads a procession of fathers carrying the youngest children into town. These boys have joined during the few days before the *Zomu*'s entrance and the official closing of the bush, so they have spent only about ten days to two weeks in the initiation village. Even these children wear the gowns and hats and have their bodies covered with white chalk.

After the youngest are taken to their individual quarters, the formal procession begins. The *kwelebah* enters, followed by the Zo hierarchy led by Bakolleah, the Zo in charge of speaking on behalf of the priesthood. Behind the Zo are the boys, being led by the new *Folpah*, who the previous evening had been given the name "Folpah" by the *ngamu*. The last to leave is the *Zomu*. The procession goes first to the house of Chief Vallai. He briefly greets them and gives a short blessing. He says that he will have something to say the next day. The boys are then led into town, forming two lines, each going to a different *taa*. Once inside their *taa*, the boys are taken to their respective *kolii*. There, the men of the quarter place woven mats in front of all the houses. The boys sit, covering up the fronts of all the houses in the area. They are told to sit with their heads still bowed so that the women will have difficulty identifying them. Once the boys are seated, the women may walk up and locate their children. Although they may stand before their boys and shout praises, they are still unable to talk directly to them. That evening, the boys sleep together in half-built houses at the outskirts of each *koli*.

The next morning, the boys are given hot water and rice. They then dress and prepare themselves to be presented formally to Chief Vallai. In the late morning, the procession begins. The boys once again walk in lines throughout the community, led by their respective *koli* leaders. They all pass by the house of Vallai and are then seated in the *kolii* immediately adjacent to Vallai's section of Zokolomii *koli*.

Virtually every man in town comes and sits in front of Vallai's house. The chief and the major elders in town sit next to the door. On the right, all the Zo in the hierarchy sit together, with Bakolleah Gbonopili, the Zo spokesman, and Mulbah Sumo Jackollie, the head Zo, in the front. Across from them sit the visitors from Guinea. My informant cameramen and assistants with tape recorders situate themselves surrounding the area. They always make sure that they are lower than the speakers, for to take a position equal to or above them would be an act of disrespect. After waiting for nearly an hour, Bakolleah Gbonopili stands up and calls two elders, Nyalong and Bilong, and presents them each with a country cloth gown. Both carry long metal hooks used in the scarification of the initiates. The men put on the gowns and then take a seat to the side of the Zo. Bakolleah Gbonopili then begins his oratory:

BAKOLLEAH: I reach the matter to the *kwelebah*, Flumo [Vallai's son], Lubulah Kollie for Banamii quarter, Kaboku for Yamii quarter—
VALLAI: Why is your back turned to me? I am the main person, and you should speak directly to me by facing this way.
BAKOLLEAH: (Turning toward Vallai) I also reach the matter to Gboko for Banya quarter, Mulbah Muwulu for Banamii quarter, to Sumo Wula who is the *kwelebah* for the men and Jakaa who is the women's *kwelebah*. I reach it to the ancestors. It also reaches to all the men and women in town who participated in the Poro society. Especially to the women who gave the men the blessings to be successful in what we are doing. It is through their blessings that the men were successful in their parts they played in Poro. I reach the matter to the blacksmith, to the Mina Zo, to the Moling Zo, to the Sande Zo, to the Jasii Zo, and to Torka-long who is the head of the Iron. I reach it to Moninghwulu who is head of the Guineans that came here to join Poro. I reach the matter to all and to whom matters should be reached to Su-cromu. I reach it to the representatives of the Zo who have come from Kpaiyea and the other Vavala towns. I reach it to the head Zo of Sangoli and the head Zo of Gbaling. The matter also reaches to the Loma people. The boys went into the bush hap-pily and came back into town happily. We should end everything happily in the name of the Lord.
EVERYONE: *Mayna.*
BAKOLLEAH: The boys that joined the society and that have come back to town, they should all behave properly and none of them should make us shamed, in the name of the Lord.
EVERYONE: *Mayna.*
BAKOLLEAH: Let no snake bite any of them; none of them should fall from a plam tree; no one should drown in a river; and when any one of them has a child, he should grow and add to the society in the name of the Lord.
EVERYONE: *Mayna.*

BAKOLLEAH: If any of them should take a position in the government, the person should get a high post and some money, bring it home, and add to the welfare of the family in the name of the Lord.

EVERYONE: *Mayna.*

BAKOLLEAH: The government is an instrument of the state and is an instrument of the society. We thank Mr. Mulbah, who is now the assistant head nurse, for the role he played in the opening of the hospital. He was the first nurse here, in fact. We thank you. May you hold your job forever. Mulbah should have some children and should move in the direction of his finger [his children should always follow his direction and advice] in the name of the Lord.

EVERYONE: *Mayna.*

BAKOLLEAH: I reach the matter to Vallai.

(Several men from Sangoli and Gbling enter the area.)

BAKOLLEAH: Let me now repeat myself. I want to thank the people of Sangoli and Gbling who helped us. They gathered together and appointed Chief Vallai's son, Flumo, to take his place when he dies. I thank you. Flumo is all of our son and now that they went to Sucron and came down and have appointed Flumo as the head to replace his father. Flumo should live as long as hunger and as long as poverty forever and ever. God help Flumo exercise his power over Vavala, Gbling, and Sangoli and do things in the favor of the majority. I reach it again to Vallai through the *kwelebah* and to the *loi kalong*. Since the Poro business, Vallai has always given blessing and the blessings have come through. Now he has done it again. This is really a great one because the number is so large. Vallai should always give his blessing, and the blessing should always work. So I am personally giving one dollar to Chief Vallai as a token for his good blessings.

(One of the elders walks up to Bakolleah and whispers in his ear that he has forgotten to mention James Flumo, the clan chief of Vavala clan.)

BAKOLLEAH: I am sorry. I have so many places to reach the matter that whenever I forget you should remind me, so I am going back to reach it to the clan chief, James Flumo. I also reach the matter to Folpahzoi and his assistant town chief, Walawulu. Now that they have been appointed and elected to move about for the town and Flumo is negotiating for the clan wherever they are

traveling and whenever they are traveling, they should be safe
and should have strong legs to travel. In the name of the Lord.

EVERYONE: *Mayna.*

KABOKU: (Walks up to Bakolleah) Do not forget the Guinean people.

SUMO: He has already reached it to them.

VALLAI: If Bakolleah does not reach it everywhere, I will; Vallai will
do it. They have made so many Poro *kuu*, but this *kuu* is a real
big one.

BAKOLLEAH: *Kwelebah*, I reach it to you and to our *ngala*, who are
the *loi kalong*. The boys who were given to Nyalong, I gave it to
him, and Nyalong gave them to Bilong, and Bilong gave it to the
kwelebah, and then they went to the bush. We have brought
them back to town. When the boys were presented to me, they
were presented with a kola, and now that we have brought these
boys back, I cannot keep the kola; I give it back to Vallai. This
is the same kola. Vallai, here are the boys. They are all healthy
and the number of boys that went to bush, all of them returned
safely.

MULBAH SUMO JACKOLLIE [the head Zo]: The number of boys was
1,247. All of them returned to town safely.

KWELEBAH: Before Vallai returns this bowl [containing the ritual
kola], it should be filled with money.

VALLAI: That is all right.

KWELEBAH: The bowl is a symbol for success.

(Vallai stands up to give his remarks.)

VALLAI: I thank everybody. I reach it to Gbonopili and the Zo. I
thank you. You have done it. I have heard it and I appreciate it.
I reach it to Kaboku and the clan chief. I reach it to Yakpowolo
Gbing, Koha, and Yakpazuah Lopoi. They have played their
parts. I also reach it to Mulbah Muwulu, to Flumo. I reach it to
Flumo and the town. I reach it to Flumo because everyone
knows that I, Vallai, have said that Flumo will replace me. It
reaches to Yamii *koli*, Gbanya *koli*, and Banamii. To Jakolomii
too. And to whosoever matters are to be reached to in this town.
And to Hon. Briggs [the member of the Liberian House of Representatives whose home is in Sucromu]. I have already reached
it to the clan chief. It reaches to Labulah Gwiiboy and to
Gbanga. Then to Glaa. They are the main landlords. Then the
matter reaches to Bowa and his brother Totokollie. Then to the
land. Then to Vallainya, and then to the land again. Then to
Yakpawolo Sigwa and his brothers. And the matter reaches to
Mulwawulu and then back to his people from Guinea. Then the

matter reaches to Kolulah Misen. To Labulah in Bohovia in
Guinea. To every part of Guinea. And to those from Sapa. And
to whoever the matter is supposed to reach, and to everybody in
the gathering. At this time anybody that said the matter has not
been reached, to him I will ask the person if they are not a lady
or gentleman [formal terms of respect]. The matters reach to the
hunters, to the ex-soldiers, to all the ladies, to Dr. Bellman, to
Town Chief Folpahzoi and his assistant, Walawulu. They are
heading the town today. They are the governors. Anyone that
says *mayna* to a prayer should be healthy. And to now to Gbonopili, Gbonopili you have come back to town; you should sleep
in town. You should have much respect. You should have a
child. We should gather next year as we have gathered here today for a joyful occasion like the one that we are on. Now that
Flumo has been appointed to replace me, he should do and say
as I am always doing and saying in the name of the Lord.

EVERYONE: *Mayna.*

VALLAI: So far he is doing very nicely and doing what I am saying,
therefore, the blessing that I am giving him should do as I am
saying in the name of the Lord.

EVERYONE: *Mayna.*

VALLAI: His orders should be carried out. Gbonopili, I reach the matter to you, the bush that you sent them in, it was my father that
told me to send them in the bush and now they have come back
to town safely. I have reached the matter everywhere now, so I
will tell you what I have in mind to tell you. I have seen your
presentation, and I am very satisfied about it.

(Vallai presents kola to the *kwelebah* to show his appreciation
for the boys' return.)

VALLAI: To my fathers, you have always given me your children, and
I am the one that always receives them from you all. And I am
the one that can give them back to the Zo. And they have come
to present these boys back to me. So, now it reaches you, Ba-
wulu, who is the main *maling* for the entire land, and then it
reaches back to everybody in town. A person who has good action should live long, and the person that acts badly should live
only a short time. All the Guineans that came as they came
safely, they should return safely to Guinea in the name of the
Lord.

EVERYONE: *Mayna.*

VALLAI: The Guineans should have children, and their children
should not be blind, they should be able to hear, and they should

be intelligent. And they should do what their parents are doing in the name of the Lord.

EVERYONE: *Mayna.*

VALLAI: The person should not be paralyzed, the person should not have hernia; and if anyone should try to spoil the friendship between the Guineans and the Liberians, the person should be disgraced in the name of the Lord. The person should not even be successful. If the person tries to do it, the people should expose him before he does it. The Guineans are our *ngala*, and the person who tries to spoil between the Guineans and the Liberians, if that person looks at the sky, the ground, if the person sucks breasts, or eats anything from a woman, or if the person walk on the road and meets a woman or a man, the person should die. If the person sleeps in a house, the person should die. I am doing as my father said. Right now it reach to the Zo. Here is five dollars for the man who I called in the morning. The man used to cut sand [divine] for the Poro society to tell the fortunes and misfortunes in advance. However, we are not doing as we used to do; in situations like this we used to give Zo clothes to wear. But right now is a very hard situation. Since we cannot give you all clothes, here is forty dollars. Now to Yakpawolo Gbing, Kokula Boipoi, and Koha, you should live as long as hunger, you should have a lot of respect; here is five dollars for the three of you from my fathers. I hope that you are understanding and remembering. Now to Bakolleah Gbonopili, the *kwelebah* has done very well; here is a dollar and fifty cents for him. To Bakolleah again and his colleagues, here is a dollar and fifty cents for the Zo singers. Anyone who talks to a blessing should live long. The reason why I am happy is that you all have listened to what I have said and try to do as I tell you to do. I have never been shamed, and this is one of the main *meni* of the Poro situation this year. This is the one I am satisfied with of all the other ones that you have done. Also, the Guineans that went in the bush are even more than the boys from Sucromu and I am very happy that there is no palaver between the Guineans and the Liberians. To all the Guineans that came, who was hurt or whose feeling was hurt?

GUINEANS: (In concert) No one.

VALLAI: Now the society is over, and you people from Guinea are our uncles. We are for you people. But if you get a woman and build a house and put the woman in the house and make her the head wife, if she goes somewhere and comes back, she gets the blessing for the entire house. And you Guineans have built the house, and I, Vallai, am the head wife today, so I get the blessing right now for everybody. [As the Guineans are considered to be the founders of the Poro, Vallai is the recipient of their ancestor's work. Thus, he is the head wife who takes care of the house, viz., the community where the Poro has initiation rituals.] I will give you the blessing. My father instructed me to give you the blessing. I have tried and here is the chance.

(At that, Vallai bows on his knees before the Guineans. The *kwelebah* rings his bell loudly, and the Zo singers chant.)

VALLAI: And now it reaches you, Mulbah Wuwulu and Labulah. I do not want you to go back to Guinea and you say that I did not reach the matter to you. A hunter is not to miss because he does not shoot to miss. We went somewhere sometime ago, and we came back and told us something: "Oh, how can they treat us like that. We all went and came back, and then you forgot about us and didn't call our names." That is why I am saying your names outside for everybody to hear it. So that all will hear it and understand it. However, I have begged in advance on behalf of the Zo and give a dollar as kola and extend apology. It was not the fault of the Zo. They are all small boys. I am still begging all of you on behalf of them. Forget what happened over there. We are all one. No one can stand for another cheating. Poro or Sande misfortune should miss them.

MULBAH: (Speaking for the Guineans) If your wife does good work for you, you tie a *lappa* on her as a reward. A child cannot talk about the way he was born. You can tell a person that we were once friends, but we are not friendly again. But you cannot tell a person that he was once born, but are not born again. Kindness requires praise [or memory]. A person's eye owns the sun; it shows it as it appears. They lighted our eyes. [Friendship is temporary, but membership in the Poro is forever.]

(In so asserting, he formally accepts Vallai's tribute.)

The matter is then "reached back" to Vallai. He gives blessings for all who attend the presentation. Then everyone leaves the compound, and the boys, sitting in the adjacent areas, are led back to their respective quarters. The members of the Zo hierarchy then walk in their final procession throughout the community. They stop at each house that has given an initiate to the society. Bakolleah Gbonopili holds the kola gourd up to those they greet and accepts a money tribute from them. In several cases, the Zo are also presented with gifts of cane juice, which they drink with the donor. When they finish their walk, they go into the Zo fence, where they divide the money between them. The ability to collect in this manner is the result of Bakolleah's request of Vallai that before the bowl is returned, "it should be filled with money."

The boys all return to their quarters and sit on the mats in front of each of the houses. In the late afternoon they are divided into smaller family units and marched through the community by their fathers or other sponsors. That evening everyone in town except the initiates and young women go to bed early. The town is turned over to the initiates and the young women for dancing and festivity. The boys play Highlife records on battery record players and dance with the girls, who are all dressed in new clothes sewn especially for this occasion.

During the following week, the boys are led about the community in family processions to the homes of their *ngala* to receive tribute in the form of clothes and money. Many are taken to the farming villages of the other towns in the clan. There are feasts that include varieties of meats and much drinking of palm wine and cane juice. The boys are presented to the hosts dressed in their gowns and hats. They march with bowed heads in a single-file procession in the same manner as they first enter town. After almost two weeks of celebration, the *Zomu* is told to remove his hat, and then the other initiates are free to remove their own (although some continue to wear their costumes for several more weeks for additional presentations to family members in distant communities).

The metaphors of pregnancy and rebirth transform the initiates from things in the bush (bush-things, or *noi sheng*), which include the various types of devils, to living human beings. The evening of the day the *ngamu* came to town and announced that his wife was in labor and would soon deliver, the boys were led from the *weiawoli* to an area just outside of town. There they waited in silence for the presence of *ngamu*. The formal ritual began with the *ngamu* announcing his walk through town. He stated first the necessity of having to greet Vallai because the "*loi kalong* owns the Zo and the Zo owns the devil. The devil cannot control the Zo." In so doing, the *ngamu* performer recited the power relations that exist between the town and the society. The Poro protects the community and represents it in dealings with other towns. It does so, however, only under the authority of the owner of the land, who represents the entire secular ruling structure. Although very often the landlord is the town chief, he need not be. As landlord, Vallai controlled more than the boundaries of Sucromu. He also represented the various towns in Guinea that, by coming to Sucromu to join the Poro, also recognized his position and authority. This is apparent in Bakolleah Gbonopili's speech discussed later.

When the *ngamu* approached Vallai, he said that there were "many medicines in the *mortar*." This parable is usually said when the *ngamu* moves on to another house after greeting an elder. In this case, he used it instead to inform Vallai not only of his presence in town but that were other matters to attend to: the rebirth performance. Through a parable the *ngamu* informed Vallai that the initiates were all safe: "the thing that can kill a person's child, mine is not going." *Ngamu* then used another parable, "A person that chases from one frog to another can cause a person to remain in frog water," to state that the time for ending the initiations had come. This parable is normally used as a warning given to a man who chases after so many women that he will never be able to attain a wife. In this case, however, the *ngamu*'s reference was to his continually seeking more initiates to kill, and therefore if he continued he would not be able to enjoy their rebirth into the community. The *ngamu* used the mortar and frog parables differently from their usual applications, and so they became living metaphors in Ricouer's (1977) sense. They had a particular rhetorical effect absent from their other applications.

The parables thus established that the situation was special and that all communication must be interpreted differently from other occasions when the *ngamu* makes an appearance. The *ngamu* established the sacred nature of the occasion a second time when he warned those who accompanied him on his walk that "the hook dropped by me is carefulness. An amateur Zo does not know leaves. The *ngamu*'s pregnancy is on you; keep away from it." The hook in this case refers to the hand of the *ngamu*, which is an actual hook at the end of his arm. This is also representative of the hook used to perform the scarification during the first phase of the initiation process. Thus, this statement means that the *ngamu*'s acts are all meaningful and planned. The reference to the "amateur does not know leaves" means that, although those around the *ngamu* may have the right as members to be near, they had best have protections if they do anything to disturb the *ngamu* in his performance during the period when "the *ngamu*'s pregnancy is on you." The formulation of a condition being "on" someone is normally used to express states of hunger (*pulu kaa ma*, "hunger is on me") or illness (*kwelea kaa ma*, "sickness is on me"). Thus in the case of the pregnancy, the condition is "on" the entire community, meaning that a dangerous condition affecting the health or well-being of the community prevails. This statement thus created an atmosphere of formality that is noticeably different from the other performances of *ngamu* throughout the initiation period. In the ritual presented at the beginning of this chapter, the *ngamu* continually had to warn those that accompanied him about town to go to bed if they were drunk to avoid trouble. Now all the men who surrounded the *ngamu* moved quietly. The only noise they made was the recitation of the appropriate chant in the call–response pattern that was expected of all members.

As the *ngamu* walked to the area of town where the initiates were waiting, he entered into a metaphorical dialogue with the *yabolo*, or singer. Both the *yabolo*'s songs and the *ngamu*'s announcements, which were translated by the *kwelebah*, contained advice and gave warnings about what is correct behavior for a Poro member. As they walked, the *ngamu* shouted threats, as well as his praises for those who respect Zo *meni*. The *yabolo* sang the part of women, characterizing the men's belief of what the women experienced throughout the initiation process. The songs lamented that "they are afraid of death. Mine did not wash the traveling clothes" (i.e., the initiates were so afraid that they had no time to prepare for their "trip" to the society fence), and "Mine is in the hands of a learning Zo. They tied me until they carried my child away" (i.e., that the woman's child is not being protected by a Zo who has knowledge of medicines and that her son was taken away from her by force).

When the *ngamu* reached the line of initiates, he called out, "Extend my words to Welikaw's son [Flumo]. There are only eleven months." Now it was the *ngamu* who used the expression 'ten plus one' as Flumo had done the month before. This was the *ngamu*'s formal proclamation to Flumo, who was now in the position of his father as *loi kalong*, that the rebirth ritual was about to begin. The boys would leave the bush the following day. The *ngamu* then stated that "the coming out night says morning. Spying cannot see it unless you look on it." Although the initiates would appear the next day, the "coming out" had to take place in the evening because all Zo *meni* must take place in the night. The *kwelebah* answered the *ngamu*'s statement with the parable "Twins cannot be in the sun's stomach." This was a double assertion that the coming out and the rebirth cannot take place at the same time and that the Poro and Sande initiations cannot occur together. With that, the *ngamu* began to name the new initiates.

The *ngamu* gave to each boy a series of names of things from the bush, which were in turn rejected by the father or sponsor of the initiate. The *ngamu* called worm, frog, insect, and caterpiller as names of bush creatures and the place name of Bukolo (for members of Twasamu *taa*) or Sucron (for members of Sucronsu); the former is the steepest part of the *Folpah*'s land located on Twasa mountain, and Sucron refers to the sacred mountain of Sucronsu *taa*. By giving the bush names first, the *ngamu* referred to the ritual metaphor of the boys being born from a bush-thing, the generic name for devil. When the initiates were finally given their Poro names, they were formally predicated with human status. At the moment of the naming, they were considered reborn as humans.

The costumes the initiates wore, both when they first began the initiation process and when they returned to town after the pregnancy ritual, each contained contrasting sets of symbols. The boys were forced to wear women's head ties along with a sash that represented the cloth of the devil when they first joined. As women are forbidden to approach *ngamu*, the sash is a sign for all women to keep away. Thus, the costume contains symbols of sexual identification that contradict each other. When the initiates reentered the community after their rebirth, they also wore contradictory symbols: white chalk, which is put on infants at birth; country cloth gowns, which are the formal attire of respected elders and chiefs; and hats that covered their ears and eyes to hide their identities and that resembled the head coverings worn by men in the bush to protect their faces from the sharp sword grasses that abound there. Those symbols simultaneously presented the initiates as newly born, as in the same category as respected elders, and as having returned from the bush. Whereas the symbols worn during entrance into the initiation process represented contradictory sexual categories, those at reentry did not, for the contrast then was between symbols of youth and age within the same sexual domain.

The sets of contrasting symbols in the Poro can be compared with those used in the Sande initiation process. Before a girl joins, she is thought to be partially male. Her clitoris is considered to be a penis. In the initiation, she undergoes a clitoridectomy and thereby loses her penis and achieves her separate sexual identity. Likewise, when a boy first enters the Poro, he displays both male and female symbols. He must wear women's head ties but carry a wooden sword, and the devil's cloth, or thatch sash, is tied about his chest. When the boy is killed by the *ngamu* and placed in the wife's womb, he is reborn as a male. Whereas the mark of Sande is the loss of the clitoris/penis, the Poro marks are scars on the neck, chest, and back that signify the loss of femininity through ritual battle, death, and rebirth.

When the initiates first return to the community, although they are considered reborn Poro members, they remain in a liminal state until their formal presentation to the *loi kalong*. They can be seen but are under strict orders not to talk unless spoken to and to avoid all physical contact with women. That is why the young women who had joined the Sande during the last women's initiation had to leave town before the boys entered. They were the eligible girlfriends and potential wives, who now had to wait until the initiates were formally presented before they could approach them. That night, after the boys were presented to Vallai, the town could be turned over to the boys and young women for celebration.

The presentation of the initiates by Bakolleah Gbonopili and their acceptance by Vallai involved the formal recognition of all principals in the initiation process. Just before Bakolleah began his oration, he gave country cloth gowns to the two elders responsible for the initiates during their stay in the initiation community. Both elders held the hooked instruments used for scarification in their hands. They received their gowns, modeled them before all present, and took their seats next to the Zo. It was then that Bakolleah "reached" the matter to those involved in the initiations and to the major elders in the community. He blessed the boys by offering a scenario of a typical man's life. He prayed that they not suffer from the kinds of sicknesses and misfortunes that are common in life, that they not bring shame to the community and that, should they obtain *kwii* positions, they work for the benefit of their families. After blessing the nurse that he might keep his job forever, Bakolleah turned to Flumo, Vallai's son who had now taken over the position of *loi kalong*. Bakolleah gave a paradoxical blessing to Flumo that he should live as long as there is hunger and poverty. Inasmuch as those are considered to be the existential conditions of life, Bakolleah blessed Flumo with eternal life.

When Bakolleah presented the initiates, he revealed the concealed knowledge of the initiation rituals: that the boys were not really dead but were under the care of the Poro Zo. He said, "The boys who were given to Nyalong, I gave it to him, and Nyalong gave them to Bilong, and Bilong gave it to the *kwelebah*, and then they went to the bush. We have brought them back to town." The ritual metaphor of death was no longer used even though the day before the *ngamu* proclaimed that his wife was pregnant with the boys whom he had killed, ground up, and placed in her womb. Now, in the presentation of the boys to the *loi kalong*, the names of all those responsible for the initiates were loudly proclaimed; the objects used in the scarification were publically displayed; and to the *kwelebah* was attributed the act of bringing the initiates back to town. When the boys were first taken by the *kwelebah*, the ritual metaphors were predicated upon them: they were killed as proclaimed in the *juanay*; resurrected in *kanokowai*; and finally reborn. Upon the rebirth, the ritual drama was completed, and the metaphors were no longer relevant because the boys had now been predicated with a human status that was not metaphorical.

In Vallai's acceptance he symbolically recognized Sucromu's relations with its Guinean neighbors. Since the Poro was made illegal in Guinea, the towns Vallai named have all participatd in Sucromu's Poro and thereby acknowledge his position as *loi kalong*. They played a part in the formal transfer of power from Vallai to his son, Flumo, which took place on Sucron, Sucromu's sacred mountain. The Guineans were initially refused permission to go there, but, after a palaver, they were permitted to do so. It was to this refusal that Vallai addressed himself when he apologized to the Guinean elders and called the Sucromu Zo "small boys." The matter had long been settled behind the Poro fence; what transpired was Vallai's public portrayal of the decision reached. Vallai recognized the Guineans' part in the ritual in which the position of *loi kalong* was transferred to his son when he "reached" the matter to Labulah Gwiiboy, Gbanga, and Glaa. He referred to them as the "main landlords." Because the Zo from Guinea had to recognize Vallai as landlord in order to participate in the Sucromu Poro society, Vallai in turn paid tribute to the landlords from their respective home communities.

The Transformation from Metaphor to Reality

In this chapter, I presented translations of excerpts from three rituals that together display the kinds of shifts that occur in metaphorical reference over the course of a ritual process. The initiations follow Fernandez's (1977) definition of ritual as a series of metaphorical transformations that are sequentially predicated upon participants. The metaphors are all polysemic, and their meanings differ for the participants depending on their positions within the Poro and in the community.

Geertz (1973) considers sociology of knowledge to be really a sociology of meaning. The Poro initiation process demonstrates that the *way* meaning is expressed is as important as how it is interpreted. Everyone shares in the concealed knowledge; the sociology of knowledge concerns not so much the distribution of information as the distribution of procedures for expressing it.

The use of ritual metaphors reflects Ricouer's distinction between creative metaphor and polysemy. When the initiates first enter the initiation process, they are made to accept the part of characters in a social drama, and they thereby assume the first in a series of metaphors predicated on them during the stages in the process. Every ritual metaphor has a generalized meaning that is part of the overall image-play; yet, during the performance of certain ritual acts, metaphors are used creatively to produce specific rhetorical effects. For example, when the *ngamu* greeted Flumo on the night of the rebirth ritual, he said, "There are many medicines in the *mortar*." That parable is normally used to conclude an interaction rather than to initiate one. Its use that night directly referred to the rebirth ritual to follow the greeting of the landlord, as this represented the conclusion of the interaction that the *ngamu* had with the initiates. After the evening naming ritual was complete, the boys were turned over to the *loi kalong* and were then under his authority.

Fernandez correctly points out that what is a dead metaphor for some may be a living one for others. When a new initiate first learns that the *ngamu* is theatrically performed, the impact is as great as when the metaphor was first created. According to Ricouer's definition of living metaphor, the second use of the expression "there are eleven more months to go" was already incorporated and thus should have lacked the rhetorical effect that it had on the night when Flumo first used it. In fact, the devil did recognize the code and provided his own metaphorical response. The *ngamu*'s use of "there are eleven more months to go" carried the same message as before, but *his* use of it had as major a rhetorical effect as when the metaphor was first created.

Metaphors can only be creative by making different use of already established structural relationships between semantic categories. That explains why some metaphors work and others do not. Geertz (1973) considers this in his description of the power of metaphor, which he says "derives precisely from the interplay between the discordant meanings it symbolically coerces into a unitary conceptual framework and from the degree to which that coercion is successful in overcoming the psychic resistance such semantic tension inevitably generates in anyone in a position to receive it. When it works, a metaphor transforms a false identification into an apt analogy; when it misfires, it is a mere extravagance"[1] (p. 211). Thus, metaphors are only creative within an established normative context. When the women performed the fishnet ritual described in the last chapter, the metaphors "misfired" precisely because of the normative context. Meaning is much more than a simple relationship of signifier to signified; it includes the right to profess along with the variety of methods used to formulate the message.

In the Poro initiations, the transformation of metaphors represents what I refer to in the following chapter as a "natural history of a secret." After the presentation of the initiates to Vallai, the ritual was complete. The so-called secret was out. When the initiates were first taken into the Poro fence, they were made to give an oath promising under pain of death "not to talk it." Through being transformed by a series of ritual metaphors, they formally learned what it is to practice secrecy. The community can now rely upon the fact that they know how to follow the *ifa mo* proscription and are able to recognize its presence or absence in talk. To use the Kpelle parable cited in the introduction to this book, "The Poro man is now in their stomachs."

8
Toward a Theory of Secrecy

The characterization of secrecy and secret societies as negative, nonconsensual, and illegitimate is contradicted by secret associations that play an integral and legitimate part in the politics and daily life of a community, as do the Poro and Sande discussed in this book. The definition of secrecy as "the process of keeping other people from obtaining information you do not want them to have" (Wilsnack, 1980:471) does not account for most of the uses of secrecy in the Poro. There is much more to the expression of membership than simply a dichotomy between those who have knowledge and those who do not. I have shown how a secret can be shared by an entire community, yet spoken in specified ways that differ among categories of people who share in the knowledge. In the Poro initiations, for instance, the Zo differentiated among members, women who are members of Sande, and Mandingo, who will not join but are permitted to live in town as long as they respect the Poro's authority.

Returning to Simmel's (1950) original characterization of secrecy as a form that is invariant to content, it is possible to compare the phenomenon of secrecy across social contexts and cultures. At the beginning of this book I discussed how, by focusing on a culture where secrecy is the most pervasive concern of daily life, it is possible to examine the message forms that comprise secrets. In this study, I have analyzed the variety of forms Kpelle speakers use to communicate information not immediately observable by direct examination of the linguistic code: parables, dilemma tales, pretalk in palavers, gnomic expressions, exaggerated descriptions, allegorical accounts, and ritual metaphors. In so doing, I have treated secrecy as a communicative event. Rather than attempting to define it, I have sought to explicate its essential features by examining the forms it takes.

I have shown how Kpelle speakers locate the meaning contexts, or auspices, of social interactions, which they call *meni*. I have discussed how the categories of *meni* are either formally recognized orders of social reality, as in the case of the numerous secret-society *meni*, or ad hoc definitions of the situation that are incorporated into recognized *meni* types and last for circumscribed periods of time. I have examined how participants negotiate which *meni* will serve as the organizational grounds for an interaction, and their techniques for changing *meni* to shift status and speaking rights within a setting. I have discussed how each *meni* provides members with different methods for locating their structural position vis-à-vis others in a situation and for interpreting the intended meaning of "deep talk." After examining different kinds of "deep talk" I have analyzed how each functions as an interpretive key for discovering concealed meanings by referring to alternate conceptions and formulations of reality. In this way I have demonstrated that secrecy is an accomplished interactional phenomenon involving speaker and hearer in the use of specific interpretive procedures.

The ritual drama of the Poro initiations is the society's enactment of instructions on how to practice secrecy. It is as though the ancient Mande speakers who first invented the Poro and the Sande had read Simmel's (1950) description of secrecy and its role in social life as "the hiding of realities . . . [which result] in the possibility of a second world along the manifest world; [where] the latter is decisively influenced by the first" (p. 330). The Poro initiations involve just that; they established an alternate reality based on a "real reality." In this case, everyone in the community knows the "real reality" and collaborates in concealing it.

The founders of the Poro, however, would disagree with many of Simmel's ideas about the functions of a secret society. Simmel (1950) counters his own formulation about the significance of form over content when he maintains that the weakness of secret societies is the fact that secrets cannot remain guarded forever (p. 346). The Poro as an institution has endured for centuries. It has been able to do so not because of the secrets that it protects but because it is the very embodiment of the procedures necessary for "doing" secrecy. The society's rituals are an expression of the form of secrecy rather than its content. The society has survived because of its concern with form.

Simmel (1950) argues that the essence of the secret society is its autonomy; yet, the Poro exists only through its articulation with the secular ruling structure of the community under the landlord as its corporate representative and through its direct dependency on the Sande and its relationship to the various secret associations subsidiary to its authority. For Simmel, the rituals of a secret society reflect "a measure of freedom and severance from society at large" (p. 361). In the Poro,

however, the severance is only metaphorical because everyone, whether
or not a direct participant in the ritual play, has a specified role to perform
in the process.

Simmel (1950) was aware of the Poro or Poro–like peoples when he
referred to "African nature groups." He described the purpose of seclusion and masking in African secret societies as a way of differentiating
men from women:

> Whenever their members act in this capacity, they appear in
> masks, and women are usually forbidden on severe penalty to
> approach them. Yet sometimes women succeed in discovering
> the secret that the horrible apparitions are not ghosts, but their
> husbands. When this happens, the orders often lose their whole
> significance and become harmless mummeries. (p. 364)

Contrary to Simmel, the women know all along that the "horrible apparitions" are really their husbands. The enactment of Poro rituals serves to
establish the ways in which that concealed information is communicated.
It provides instruction in how to deal with any concealed information by
proffering various types of message forms that can legitimately be used to
express it. It offers methods for mentioning the unmentionable.

The content of the Poro secret is publicly expressed at the end of the
ritual process when the initiates are formally presented to the landlord.
At that time, the ritual metaphors used throughout the process are no
longer relevant. The secret is out that the boys were not really killed by
the devil, ground up, and placed in the wife's womb but were instead
living in a community under the supervision of the Poro Zo somewhere in
the forest. In contrast, during the ritual process, it was crucial that
everyone make appropriate use of the metaphors pertaining to his or her
respective category of participation in the ritual. In this way the women's
part in the initiation process is as crucial as that of the Poro Zo, a fact
made explicit when the Zo *nang*, Bakolleah Gbonopili, blessed the
women for their participation.

The initiates themselves know from the beginning that they are not
really going to die when they encounter the *ngamu* behind the Poro fence
that first morning. It is important, nevertheless, that they publicly declare
the existence of their forthcoming battle by promising to bring parts of
the *ngamu* back to the community, for in so doing, the ritual metaphor of
warrior-hunter is predicated upon them. Then, the metaphor of death is
predicated when they are scarred to signify their being ground up in the
mouth of the *ngamu*. Next, the metaphor of the *ngamu* is put on them as
they reside inside the initiation community and perform ritual acts in the
ngamu's name. In so doing they formally recognize that the *ngamu* stands

for the membership of the society. They learn the nature of power relationships within the community as expressed by the *ngamu* at the end of the ritual process when he says that the Zo controls the *ngamu*, and the landlord controls the Zo.

The examination of the Poro initiations demonstrates that Simmel's (1950) claim that "the whole separateness becomes invalid once the secret of the mask is broken . . . the secret society loses its inner significance along with its means and its expression" (p. 364) is incorrect. The secret of the mask is known all along. When the Guinean government declared the Poro illegal, it had the membership and Zo priesthood display their ritual paraphernalia before the women; yet, that act did not destroy the Poro. Over half of those who joined the Poro in Sucromu and Kpaiyea had come at great risk to Liberia from Guinea so that they might return there and practice the society as an underground association. The Poro is alive and well in Guinea in spite of the fact that officially "the secret of the mask is broken."

The Poro initiations can be considered the dramatic enactment of the natural history of a secret from its inception until the time when the need for concealment is past. In this way, the description of the relation of metaphor to ritual given by Lakoff and Johnson (1980) is applicable here. They analyze how metaphors are used in daily life, often unconsciously, and how they reflect belief systems. The metaphors we live by, say Lakoff and Johnson, are preserved in ritual, and the values "entailed by them, are propagated by ritual," making ritual "forms an indispensable part of the experiential basis for our cultural metaphorical systems. There can be no culture without ritual" (p. 234).

The women know that the boys are still alive, but to talk openly about it would jeopardize their relationships with the men. Instead, they have to use the ritual metaphors available to them whenever they want to refer to their sons and brothers in public. When the Poro Zo accused the women of exposing some of the Poro secrets by performing the fishnet ritual, they knew that the women were always aware of the existence of the initiation bush community. The other songs the women were permitted to sing all expressed that knowledge. The fishnet ritual was, however, a creative use of metaphor not under the control of the Poro Zo, so in performing it the women challenged the Poro's structural position relative to them. The Poro Zo were not angry with what was expressed but with the form of the expression.

In Western culture, access to secret information is based on the right to know and the need to know. Someone may have the right but lack the need and so be denied information he may later discover he was entitled to. This examination of the expression of secrecy in the Poro adds another dimension to the social organization of concealed knowledge. In addition to the right and need to know, this analysis shows that there are variable ways in which concealed knowledge can be formulated. Everyone may possess knowledge but have different ways in which they can express it.

I have dealt in this study more with the procedures for communicating secrets than with motivations for concealing information. Although fear of the consequences of exposing information and the terror of being so accused provide rationales for engaging in secrecy, they are not defining characteristics. As Warren and Laslett (1977) argue, fear of consequences in not enough to distinguish secrecy from privacy. One may fear the intrusion of privacy as much as the discovery of secrets.

Walter (1969) claims that terror is the primary organizing principle in social systems governed by an elite caste or by despotic rulers. He uses Harley's (1941b) description of the Poro as an instance of an elite caste using terror as a social-control mechanism and as the motivation for organizing secret societies. He characterizes the Zo's leadership as an invisible government that maintains its powers by inducing terror of masked devils, and he claims that the initiates experience great terror when they undergo their ritual deaths and rebirths. The most common emotions expressed to me by initiates were reluctance to be secluded for such an extended period and to undergo the painful scarification operation. Once the boys received their marks, they were taken to the bush community, which was, according to Flumo and other informants, a rather enjoyable experience. There was, of course, general concern that none of the boys die while in the custody of the Zo, but nowhere was there a direct expression of terror as Walter defines it: "a compound with three elements: the act or threat of violence, the emotional reaction, and the social effects" (p. 8).

It is true that the initiates are threatened not to expose the society's secrets, but the threat is more symbolic than real. The Poro and Sande are so entrenched in the local power structure that their position is unquestioned, and their authority to perform rituals resides in their acceptance by the "owner of the land," who represents the public and secular parts of the community. The Zo's authority is limited to matters considered to be Poro *meni*. There are other secret societies and numerous kinds of *meni* resulting in a complex network of interlocking memberships. The Kpelle use secrecy, not terror, as a fundamental organizing principle in their political, economic, social, religious, and interpersonal behaviors.

In this book I have examined the forms that secrets can take. I have demonstrated how the examination of the kinds of message forms used to convey and adumbrate concealed information opens up a variety of issues such as the multiple interpretations and constructions of reality that are relevant to the sociology of knowledge; the structure of discourse processes, particularly as figurative language is concerned; the polysemic and multivocalic nature of symbols in ritual; and procedures for excluding and incorporating membership. I have discussed how secrets cannot be characterized either by the contents of the concealed message or by the consequences and outcomes that follow exposure; instead, they are understood by the *way* concealed information is withheld, restricted, intentionally altered, and exposed. The practice of secrecy involves a do-not-talk-it proscription in every culture that is contradicted by the fact that secrecy is, as Simmel called it, "a sociological form" that is constituted by the very procedures whereby secrets are communicated. I have called this the paradox of secrecy. Its resolution touches upon virtually every issue relevant to the study of society.

Notes

CHAPTER ONE

INTRODUCTION

1. See Schelling (1960) for a discussion of strategies used in conflict situations and their relation to information control. Also see Wilsnack (1980) for another discussion about the relation of information control to secrecy.

2. See Sanchez (1979), who defines the metacommunicative component of messages in the manner used here.

3. See Martin (1970) for a discussion of the classic liar's paradox. Also see Cargile (1979) for an investigation of the form of paradoxes and his analysis of mistakes in describing what propositions and properties are conveyed by expressions. He demonstrates that paradoxes result from mistakes in assumptions about truth. Cargile's discussion is consistent with my treatment of the paradox involved in telling secrets.

4. There are three major linguistic groups in Liberia: Kru, Mel, and Mande. Most of the Mande- and Mel-speaking peoples have both Poro and Sande. The Kpelle are part of the Mande group along with the Mende, Loma, Gbandi, Gio, and Mano. There are five dialects of Kpelle spoken in Liberia, at least two in Guinea. Each dialect community differs from the others both linguistically and in social structure. The Fala dialect of Kpelle is spoken in the communities whose rituals I analyze in this book.

5. Although the term *devil* has pejorative connotations in our culture, it is used by members when describing the Poro bush-things and other masquerade-ritual performers in Liberian English. The various ethnic groups that have the Poro differ in the number and exact responsibilities of each bush-thing or devil. Among the Mano, Gola, Mende, Bassa, and Vai there are separate masks for the Poro and the Sande, as well as for rituals not directly associated with Poro, such as circumcision and farming rituals. Among the Kpelle and Loma there are fewer masks, and all are the possession of the Poro. The powers of the Poro bush-things are always considered greater than the authority of those in the secular ruling structure of the community.

6. See Garfinkel (1967), Garfinkel and Sacks (1970), and Psathas (1973) for discussions of the phenomenological approach in the social sciences, and see Roche (1973) for a comparison of phenomenological and ethnomethodological sociology with the methods used in conceptual analysis.

7. See Cicourel (1975) for a discussion of the abductive approach as used in cognitive sociology and ethnomethodology, which is a phenomenological adaptation from Pearce's original concept.

8. See Sacks (1972a, 1972b) for a discussion of membership-categorization devices. By these, he means the analysis of collections of categories and their rules of application.

9. See Chafe (1980) for a discussion of narrative structures and how cultural differences affect the discourse process.

10. See Bellman and Jules-Rosette (1977) for a presentation of this methodology in the analysis of informant-made video recordings and films in Liberia and Zambia.

CHAPTER TWO
THE PORO IN WEST AFRICA

1. In Kenya, secret societies were made illegal in part because of the influence that societies such as the Mau Mau had during the movement for independence. Their effectiveness was taken as an indication that secret societies represented a potential threat to the postcolonial government's ability to excercise political control over the numerous ethnic groups that had differential access to the benefits of the new society. Secret societies tended to be outlawed in those countries where the ruling ethnic elite did not have traditional secret societies or where they were never a dominant force in the local governance of their communities. This was the case in Zaire, where secret-society activity was prominent only in the eastern region. Because Mobutu's own ethnic group, the Bangala, did not have secret societies, all ethnically based, secret associations were considered a threat and were made illegal. Many of these societies, such as the Bwami, responded by going underground. This led not only to a major decline in membership but to a general deterioration of their highly developed artistic traditions.

2. See Cohen (1974, 1981) for a discussion of West African Freemasonary and its relationship to elite political structures.

3. George Way Harley was a physician-missionary-scholar who lived in Liberia for over twenty-five years. He established a major hospital and nursing training school. His books are among the most comprehensive on Liberian medicines and the structure of the Poro among the Mano-speaking peoples.

CHAPTER THREE
THE PORO AND OTHER SECRET SOCIETIES
IN THE VAVALA CLAN

1. By "ritual permission," I mean not only that the permission of the *loi kalong* is necessary but that it is given in a ritual event before the opening of the Poro bush.

2. There is the expectation that full bride-price will eventually be paid, either by the prospective husband doing work in lieu of payment or through moneys or other goods given over the course of years. See also Bledsoe (1980) for a discussion of women and marriage among the Kpelle.

3. To 'reach a matter' means formally to ask or inform someone that he or she is involved in the discussion or situation.

4. See Gibb's film *The Cows of Dolo Ken Paye* (1970), in which a cow's tail was cut off because of a farmer's anger at a chief. By cutting the tail off the cow, the animal could not be used in sacrifice, and thus its value was greatly diminished. When a cow is sacrificed, the *maling* receives the tail from the *ngala* and then uses it as a symbol of authority during palavers and family discussions.

5. See the next section of this chapter for a discussion of this society and its relation to the other Poro bush-things or "devils."

6. See Kirshenblatt-Gimblett (1976) for a discussion of types of speech play in various cultures.

7. Welmers reflects a Western interpretive bias that magic is always accomplished through deception. Instead, the so-called trick is better considered to be member's knowledge that is obtained in the course of ritual activity and instruction. When I first began my research in Liberia, I learned medicines from a Zo named Kutupu in a community near Cuttington College, about 120 miles in the interior. Kutupu ran a medicine practice analogous to Western mission hospitals. He sat on a raised pedestal with his patients seated before him. Each, in turn, would come to the front and state his troubles. Kutupu would ask for a sum of money (which varied with the distance traveled by the seeker) and place it under the cover of the Koran. He then placed a medicine horn, or *mina*, on top of the book and discussed the patient's troubles with him or her. After a while, he picked up the book and used it as an oracle. He would say, "If the person's troubles are the result of his/her having broken a food taboo, then the money should disappear." He then passed the book three times around his back for a woman and four for a man. If the money was still there, he would choose another cause: "If the troubles are the result of someone making bad medicine" or "that an evil *jina* (malefic spirit) is the problem." Kutupu then turned the book behind his back so that the other side was face up. When he opened the book the money seemed to have disappeared. Then he would discuss how to cure the patient; to show the effectiveness of the diagnosis, he made the money reappear by again turning the book behind his back. Because I was "apprenticing" under Kutupu, I sat to his side and was able to see how he performed his oracle.

A short time after having learned how Kutupu did his divination, I visited some Kpelle college students. One asked me what I had learned from Kutupu. I showed him the oracle. All present were astonished that I made the money disappear, and no one appeared to notice when I turned the book behind my back. Finally, I announced how I made the money disappear. Instead of destroying the illusion that I created, my friend stated, "Yes, of course, but Kutupu knows *when* to turn the book." The fact that I showed them the trick did not disturb their belief in the oracle.

8. See Murphey (1976) for a discussion of the Snake Society among the

Kakataa Kpelle in the Fuama Chiefdom. They appear to place the society within the Poro structure similar to the Mano. This may be due to the nearness of the Mano to this group of Kpelle speakers.

CHAPTER FOUR
THE CONCEPT OF SECRECY IN SECRET SOCIETIES

1. For Schutz, each order is characterized by a specific tension of consciousness analogous to Bergson's "attention a la vie," a specific epoche or suspension of doubt, a prevalent form of spontaneity, a specific form of experiencing oneself, a specific form of sociality, and a specific time perspective.

2. See Gurwitsch (1964) for his critique of Schutz as being overly psychologistic in his characterization of orders of reality. See also Bellman (1975) for a discussion of Kpelle orders of reality following Gurwitsch's revision of Schutz.

3. Goffman, in *Frame Analysis* (1974) discussed Schutz's concept of orders of reality and assumed an existential approach consistent with Gurwitsch.

4. There has been much discussion about the universality of the simplest systematics of turn taking (see Sherzer, 1974). Sacks, Schegloff, and Jefferson (1974) postulate a set of context-sensitive rules applicable in every culture. They argue that, though the application of the rules may differ because of differing cultural conventions and situational factors, these differences are all analyzable using the formal rules they describe.

5. See Bellman (1975) and Harley (1941a) for discussions of traditional Liberian medicines and their relation to secret societies.

CHAPTER FIVE
SECRETS AS TEXTS: THE MESSAGE FORMS OF DEEP TALK

1. See Garfinkel and Sacks (1970) for an analysis of conversational formulations. My analysis of how the mentioning of *meni* has a rhetorical function within a speech event is consistent with their discussion of the "work" of formulations in discourse.

2. This is also called "inside Kpelle talk." See Murphey (1976) and Kulah (1973) for discussions of Kpelle proverbs and their logical structures. According to Murphey, Kpelle proverbs always relate to an inside–outside comparison. Hence, the expression used to describe the location of the Poro initiates while they are in the forest village, "inside the devil's stomach," is consistent with that structure.

3. Compare with Cicourel's (1974) analysis of interpretive procedures. His study is of the formal structures, as Garfinkel (1967) called them, that constitute practical reasoning. Here I use *procedures* to refer to the particular methods speakers consciously use to understand "deep talk." They are socially learned practices and make use of the cognitive interpretive procedures that Cicourel and Garfinkel write about.

4. See Bellman (1975) for a critique of Schutz's analysis of dreams using the Kpelle concept as comparative data.

5. There are several methods of divining practiced. Sand cutting involves the diviner moving a stick across sand and putting the resulting piles into a sequential order resembling some aspects of the *Ifa* oracle in Nigeria. Other types of divining include the *faa sale* oracle of the Iron Society discussed earlier.

6. This is consistent with the literature on the sociology of confessions (Jules-Rosette, 1975).

7. Searle (1979) used this as a basis for determining what is actually a metaphor. He provides a detailed analysis of what is logically implied in different metaphoric forms within speech acts.

8. See Bok (1979) for a typology of kinds of lies and their various philosophic implications.

9. Halliday and Hansan (1976) and Bernstein (1974) call such talk *exophoric*. Exophoric reference points to something in the situational context. See also Ben-Amos (1975) for types of exophoric genre in Africa folklore.

10. See the explanation of the translation process at the end of the Introduction.

CHAPTER SIX
SECRETS AND THE INITIATION RITUAL

1. The so-called hermeneutical circle was developed first by Gadamer (1975), following Heidegger (1962), to refer to the interpretive paradox involved where "any interpretation which is to contribute understanding, must already have understood what it is to be interpreted" (Gadamer, 1975:259). See also Palmer (1970) and Bleicher (1980) for discussion of the development of the concept and its central place in interpretive philosophy. See also Giddens (1976) for a different view that both contributes to and critiques hermeneutical and phenomenological social science theory.

2. The Highlife recordings from Zaire and Nigeria are also popular in Liberia, but the music from Kenya tends to dominate the market.

3. See Rumelhardt (1975) for a discussion of story schemata and the development of what is now referred to in the cognitive psychological literature as story grammars.

4. The history of the theory of metaphor goes back as far as Western philosophic inquiry. It is only recently, however, that the concept of metaphor has seriously been treated in the social sciences. See Max Black (1962) for a discussion of the history and operation of metaphor especially as it relates to scientific models. See Fernandez (1974) for a presentation of metaphor as it pertains to ritual symbolism and the relation of metaphor to culture. See also Sapir and Crocker (1977) for a set of excellent essays on the use of metaphor in rhetoric. See Ricouer (1977) for a presentation of the history of concern with metaphor, a critique of approaches, and his own rhetorical theory, from which I borrowed, of the distinction between metaphor and its creative applications.

CHAPTER SEVEN
MENTIONING THE UNMENTIONABLE

1. This quotation comes from Geertz's discussion of Sutton's example of the failure of the metaphor "slave labor law" for the Taft-Hartley Labor Act. The analogy was that the labor policy of the Republican party, as represented in the act, was forced labor. Forced labor was linked to the forced labor attributed to the so-called slave labor camps in Russia under Stalin. The associations were in discord with the belief system of the labor movement and thus the metaphor "misfired."

Bibliography

Adams, Monni (ed.)
1980   *Ethnologische Zeitschrift.* Bern: Peter Lang.
Adler, Patricia; and Adler, Peter
1980   The irony of secrecy in the drug world. *Urban Life* 8 (4):447–466.
Albert, Ethel M.
1972   Culture patterning of speech behavior in Burundi. In *Directions in sociolinguistics: The ethnography of communication*, ed. John Gumperz and Dell Hymes, pp. 72–105. New York: Holt, Rinehart & Winston.
Arewa, Ojo; and Shreve, G. M.
1975   *The genesis of structures in African narrative.* New York: Conch.
Bascom, William
1975   *African dilemma tales.* The Hague: Mouton.
Bellman, Beryl L.
1975   *Village of curers and assassins: On the production of Fala Kpelle cosmological categories.* The Hague: Mouton.
1977   Ethnohermeneutics: On the interpretation of intended meaning in Kpelle accounts. In *Language and thought*, ed. William McCormack and Stephen Wurm, pp. 271–282. The Hague: Mouton.
1979   The social organization of knowledge in Kpelle ritual. In *The new religions of Africa*, ed. Bennetta Jules-Rosette, Norwood, N.J.: Ablex.
Bellman, Beryl L.; and Jules-Rosette, Bennetta
1977   *A paradigm for looking: Cross-cultural research with visual media.* Norwood, N.J.: Ablex.
Ben-Amos, Dan (ed.)
1975   *Folklore genres.* Austin, Tex.: University of Texas Press.
Bernstein, Basil
1974   *Class, codes and control: Theoretical studies towards a sociology of language.* New York: Schocken.

Black, Mary
   1969   Eliciting folk taxonomies in Ojibwa. In *Cognitive anthropology*, ed.
           Stephen Tyler. New York: Holt, Rinehart & Winston.
Black, Max
   1962   *Models and metaphors*. Ithaca, N.Y.: Cornell University Press.
Bledsoe, Caroline H.
   1980   *Women and marriage in Kpelle society*. Stanford, Calif.: Stanford
           University Press.
Bleicher, Josef
   1980   *Contemporary hermeneutics*. London: Routledge & Kegan Paul.
Bok, Sissela
   1979   *Lying: Moral choice in public and private life*. New York: Random
           House, Vintage.
Bonacich, Phillip
   1976   Secrecy and solidarity. *Sociometry* 39:200–208.
Cargile, James
   1979   *Paradoxes: A study in form and predication*. London: Cambridge
           University Press.
Chafe, Wallace
   1980   The deployment of consciousness in the predication of a narrative. In
           *The pear stories: Cognitive, cultural, and linguistic aspects of narrative
           production*, ed. Wallace Chafe, pp. 9–50. Norwood, N.J.: Ablex.
Chomsky, Noam
   1965   *Aspects of a theory of syntax*. Cambridge, Mass.: MIT Press.
Chrisman, Noel J.
   1974   Middle class communitas: The Fraternal Order of the Badgers. *Ethos*
           2:356–376
Cicourel, Aaron V.
   1974   *Cognitive sociology*. New York: Free Press.
   1975   Discourse and text: Cognitive and linguistic processes in studies of
           social structure. In *Versus: Quaderni di Studi Semiotici*.
Cohen, Abner
   1974   The politics of ritual secrecy. *Man* 6:427–448.
   1981   *The politics of elite culture*. Berkeley and Los Angeles: University of
           California Press.
Cole, M; Gay, John; Glick, Joseph; and Sharp, D.
   1971   *The cultural context of learning and thinking*. New York: Basic Books.
Coser, Lewis
   1956   *The functions of social conflict*. New York: Free Press.
   1963   The dysfunctions of military secrecy. *Social Problems* 11:13–21.
d'Azevdo, Warren
   1962   Some historical problems in the delineation of a central west Atlantic
           region. *Annals of New York Academy of Sciences* 96:512–538.
   1965   *The artist archtype in Gola culture*. Desert Research Institute Occa-
           sional Paper no. 14. Reno: University of Nevada.
   1973a   Mask makers and myth in western Liberia. In *Primitive art and society*,

ed. A. Forge, pp. 126–150. London and New York: Oxford University Press.

1973b Sources of Gola artistry. In *The traditional artist in African societies*, ed. Warren d'Azevedo, pp. 282–340. Bloomington: Indiana University Press.

Erchack, Gerald M.

1977 *Full respect: Kpelle children in adaptation.* New Haven, Conn.: HRAF, Human Relations Area Files.

Fernandez, James W.

1971 Persuasions and performances: Of the beast in everybody and metaphors of everyman. In *Myth, symbol and culture*, ed. Clifford Geertz, pp. 39–60. New York: Norton.

1974 The mission of metaphor in expressive culture. *Current Anthropology* 15:119–145.

1977 The performance of ritual metaphors. In *The social use of metaphor*, ed. David Sapir and J. Christopher Crocker, pp. 100–131. Philadelphia: University of Pennsylvania Press.

Fischer, Eberhard

1980 Mask rituals among the Dan. In *Ethnologische Zeitschrift*, ed. Monni Adams. Bern: Peter Lang.

Fulton, Robert

1972 The political functions of Poro in Kpelle society. *American Anthropologist* 74:1218–1233.

Gadamer, Hans-Georg

1975 *Truth and method.* New York: Seabury.

Garfinkel, Harold

1963 Conception of experiments with "trust" as a condition of stable concerted actions. In *Motivation and social interaction*, ed. O. J. Harvey, pp. 183–238. New York: Ronald.

1967 *Studies in ethnomethodology.* Englewood Cliffs, N.J.: Prentice-Hall.

Garfinkel, Harold; and Sacks, Harvey

1970 On formal structures of practical actions. In *Theoretical sociology*, ed. John McKinney and Edward Tiryakian, pp. 337–366. New York: Appelton-Century-Crofts.

Gay, John

1971 Kpelle uses of Kpelle logic. *Liberian Research Association Journal* 3 (2):40–50.

1973 *Red dust on green leaves.* Thompson, Conn.: InterCulture.

Geertz, Clifford

1973 Ideology as a cultural system. In idem, *The interpretation of cultures*, pp. 193–233. New York: Basic Books.

Gibbs, James L., Jr.

1962 Poro values in courtroom procedures in a Kpelle chiefdom. *Southwestern Journal of Anthropology* 19:9–20.

1963a The Kpelle moot: A therapeutic model for informal settlement of disputes. *Africa* 11:1–11.

1963b   Marital instability among the Kpelle: Towards a theory of epainog-
         amy. *American Anthropologist* 65:552–573.
1965   The Kpelle of Liberia. In *Peoples of Africa*, ed. James L. Gibbs, pp.
         New York: Holt, Rinehart & Winston.
1970   *The cows of Dolo Ken Paye*. Film. New York: Holt, Rinehart &
         Winston.
Giddens, Anthony
1976   *The rules of sociological method*. New York: Basic Books.
Glaze, Anita
1975   Woman, power and art in a Senafor village. *African Arts* 75:25–91.
Goffman, Erving
1963   *Behavior in public places*. New York: Free Press.
1969   *Strategic interaction*. Philadelphia: University of Pennsylvania Press.
1971   *Relations in public: Microstudies of the public order*. New York: Basic
         Books.
1974   *Frame analysis*. New York: Harper & Row, Colophon.
Goldwater, R.
1964   *Senufo sculpture from West Africa*. Greenwich, Conn.: New York
         Graphic Society.
Gurwitsch, Aron
1964   *The field of consciousness*. Pittsburgh: Duquesne University Press.
Halliday, M. A.; and Hansan, R.
1976   *Cohesion in English*. London: Longmans, Green.
Harley, George Way
1941a   *Native African medicine with special reference to its practice in the Mano
         tribe of Liberia*. Cambridge, Mass.: Harvard University Press.
1941b   *Notes on the Poro in Liberia*. Peabody Museum Papers, vol. 19, no. 2.
         Cambridge, Mass.: Peabody Museum.
1950   *Masks as agents of social control in Northeast Liberia*. Peabody
         Museum Papers, vol. 32, no. 2. Cambridge, Mass.: Peabody Museum.
Harris, W.; and Sawyer, H.
1968   *The springs of Mende belief and conduct*. Freetown: Sierra Leone
         Press.
Heidegger, Martin
1962   *Being and time*. Trans. by J. Macquarrie and E. Robinson. New York:
         Harper & Row.
Hymes, Dell
1974   *Foundations in sociolinguistics: An ethnographic approach*. Phil-
         adelphia: University of Pennsylvania Press.
Jules-Rosette, Benneta
1975   *African apostles: Ritual and conversion in the church of John Maranke*.
         Myth, Symbol, and Ritual Series, ed. V. Turner. Ithaca, N.Y.: Cornell
         University Press.
Kermode, Frank
1979   *The genesis of secrecy*. Cambridge, Mass.: Harvard University Press.

Kirshenblatt-Gimblett, M.
1976   *Speech play*. Philadelphia: University of Pennsylvania Press.
Kulah, A. A.
1973   *The organization and learning of proverbs among the Kpelle of Liberia*.
        Ph.D. dissertation, University of California, Irvine.
Lakoff, George; and Johnson, Mark
1980   *Metaphors we live by*. Chicago: University of Chicago Press.
Little, Kenneth
1949   The role of the secret society in cultural specialization. *American
        Anthropologist* 51:199–212.
1965   The political functions of the Poro: pt. 1. *Africa* 35:349–365.
1966   The political functions of the Poro: pt. 2. *Africa* 36:62–72.
1967   *The Mende of Sierra Leone*. London: Routledge & Kegan Paul.
Lowry, Ritche P.
1972   Toward a sociology of secrecy and security system. *Social Problems*
        19:437–450.
Lyman, S. M.
1964   Chinese secret societies in the Occident: Notes and suggestions for
        research in the sociology of secrecy. *Canadian Review of Sociology and
        Anthropology* 1 (2):79–102.
McCormack, Carol
1979   The Sande: Public face of a secret society. In *The new religions of
        Africa*, ed. Bennetta Jules-Rosette, pp. 27–37. Norwood, N.J.: Ablex.
McHugh, Peter
1968   *Defining the situation: The organization of meaning in social interac-
        tion*. New York: Bobbs-Merrill.
MacKenzie, Norman
1967   *Secret societies*. London: Aldus.
Mandler, Jean M.
1977   A code in the note: The use of a story schema in retrieval. *Discourse
        Processes* 2:14–35.
Martin, Robert L. (ed.)
1970   *The paradox of the liar*. New Haven, Conn.: Yale University Press.
Metzger, Duane.
1963   Tenejapa medicine I: the curer. *Southwestern Journal of Anthropology*
        19 (2):216–234.
Murphey, William P.
1976   *A semantic and logical analysis of Kpelle proverb metaphors*. Ph.D.
        dissertation, Stanford University.
Palmer, Richard
1970   *Hermeneutics*. Evanston, Ill.: Northwestern University Press.
Ponse, Barbara
1976   Secrecy in the lesbian world. *Urban Life* 5:313–338.
Psathas, George
1973   *Phenomenological sociology*. New York: Wiley.

Ricouer, Paul
  1977   *The rule of metaphor.* Trans. by R. Czerny. Toronto: University of
          Toronto Press.
Roche, Maurice
  1973   *Phenomenology, language and the social sciences.* London and Boston:
          Routledge & Kegan Paul.
Rumelhardt, David E.
  1975   Notes on a schema for stories. In *Studies in cognitive science*, ed. D.
          Bobrow and A. Collins, pp. 211–236. New York: Academic.
Sacks, Harvey
  1972a   An initial investigation of the usability of conversational data for doing
          sociology. In *Studies in social interaction*, ed. David Sudnow, pp.
          31–74. New York: Free Press.
  1972b   On the analyzability of stories by children. In *Directions in sociolin-
          guistics: The ethnography of communication*, ed. John Gumperz and
          Dell Hymes, pp. 325–345. New York: Holt, Rinehart & Winston.
  1975   Everyone has to lie. In *Sociocultural dimensions of language use*, ed.
          Mary Sanchez and Ben Blount, pp. 57–80. New York: Academic.
Sacks, Harvey; Schegloff, Emanuel; and Jefferson, Gail
  1974   A simplest systematics for the organization of turn-taking in conversa-
          tion. *Language* 50:696–735.
Sanchez, Mary
  1979   Introduction to pt. II. In *Sociocultural dimensions of language use*, ed.
          Mary Sanchez and Ben Blount, pp. 163–176. New York: Academic.
Sapir, David
  1977   The anatomy of metaphor. In *The social use of metaphor*, ed. David
          Sapir and J. Christopher Crocker, pp. 33–66. Philadelphia: University
          of Pennsylvania Press.
Sapir, David; and Crocker, J. Christopher (eds.)
  1977   *The social use of metaphor.* Philadelphia: University of Pennsylvania
          Press.
Schaefer, Richard
  1980   The management of secrecy: The Ku Klux Klan's successful secrecy. In
          Secrecy: A cross-cultural perspective, ed. Stanton K. Tefft, pp. 161–
          177. New York: Human Sciences.
Schelling, Thomas C.
  1960   *The strategy of conflict.* Cambridge, Mass.: Harvard University Press.
Schutz, Alfred
  1962   *Collected papers*, vol. 1, *The problems of social reality.* The Hague:
          Martinus Nijhoff.
  1967   *The phenomenology of the social world.* Trans. by George Walsh.
          Evanston, Ill.: Northwestern University Press.
Schutz, Alfred; and Luckmann, Thomas
  1973   *The structures of the life-world.* Trans. by Richard Zaner and H.
          Tristram Engelhardt, Jr. Evanston, Ill.: Northwestern University
          Press.

Searle, John R.
1979   *Expression and meaning: Studies in the theory of speech acts.* Cambridge: Cambridge University Press.
Sherzer, Joel
1974   Namakke, sunmakke, kormakke: Three types of cuna speech event. In *Explorations in the ethnography of speaking*, ed. Richard Bauman and Joel Sherzer, pp. 263–282. Cambridge: Cambridge University Press.
Shils, Edward A.
1956   *The torment of secrecy: The background and consequences of American security policies.* Carbondale and Edwardsville: Southern Illinois University Press.
Siegmann, William; and Schmidt, Cynthia
1977   *Rock of the ancestors: ngamoa kawni.* Suakoko: Cuttington University College Press.
Simmel, George
1950   *The sociology of Georg Simmel.* Trans. by Kurt Wolff. New York: Macmillan.
Sutton, F. X.; Harris, S. E.; Kaysen, C.; and Toblin, J.
1956   *The American business creed.* Cambridge, Mass.: Harvard University Press.
Tefft, Stanton K.
1980a   The dimensions of secrecy: Introduction. In *Secrecy: A cross-cultural perspective*, ed. Stanton K. Tefft, pp. 13–17. New York: Human Sciences.
1980b   Secrecy as a social and political process. In *Secrecy: A cross-cultural perspective*, ed. Stanton K. Tefft, pp. 319–346. New York: Human Sciences.
Turner, Victor
1974   *Dramas, fields, and metaphors.* Ithaca, N.Y.: Cornell University Press.
Walter, Eugene V.
1969   *Terror and resistance: A study of political violence with case studies of some primitive African communities.* New York: Oxford University Press.
Warren, Carol
1974   *Identity and community in the gay world.* New York: Wiley.
Warren, Carol; and Laslett, Barbara
1977   Privacy and secrecy: A conceptual comparison. In *Privacy as a behavioral phenomenon.* Special issue of *Journal of Social Issues* (ed. Stephen T. Margulis) 33 (3):43–51.
Weber, Max
1947   *The theory of social and economic organization.* New York: Free Press.
Welmers, William E.
1948   *Spoken Kpelle.* Sanoyea: Lutheran Church of Liberia.
1949   Secret medicines, magic, and rites of the Kpelle tribe in Liberia. *Southwestern Journal of Anthropology* 5:208–243.

1962   The phonology of Kpelle. *Journal of African Languages* 1:69–93.
1971   The first course in Kpelle. In *Mathematics and logic in the Kpelle language*, ed. John Gay and William Welmers. Ibadan.
Wilsnack, Richard W.
1980   Information control: A conceptual framework for sociological analysis. *Urban Life*.

Index

Ability to know medicines, 48–50.
See also Medicine
Adjudication: devil battles and, 26–
28; lying and, 60; *meni* and, 45–46;
organizational *meni* and, 76; pretalk examples and, 68–75
Adultery, 52, 60
Albert, Ethel M., 45
Audio-recording, 11–12
Authority: central and local govern-
ments and, 26; Poro and Sande,
143; secret societies and government, 47

Baiyaemu Society, 32–33
Balasilangamu. See Sheephorn Devil
Society
Bascom, William, 63
Black, Mary, 11
Blessings, 131; gnomic, 120; with
curse, 109
Bok, Sissela, 60
Bush camp. *See* Initiation village

Chomsky, Noam, 11
Cicourel, Aaron V., 11
Circumcision, 15, 39
Clitoridectomy, 33, 135
Clothing, 23, 84; of women, 26. *See*
also Costumes

Cole, Michael, 10
Compounds, 21–22
Concealment of information: change
in definition of situation and, 75–
76; control of, 3, 5–6; Poro and,
50; right to know and, 142–143
Conversational order, sequencing,
and succession. *See Meni*, conversational formulation (meaning context of social situations)
Cooking (initiation village), 96
Coser, Lewis, 4
Costumes, 184; devil, 30–31; 93; entry ritual, 80; initiation, 82, 97,
118, 125, 126, 135, 136. *See also*
Clothing
Crime: against sacred ruling structure, 33; Poro structure and, 26

Dancing, 109, 111, 113; initiation village and, 93–94; *jinja* dance and,
81. *See also* Devil battles
Dancing-devil Society, 31–32, 40
Death: by burning, 89–90; metaphors
of, 141; Mina Society and, 34–35;
narrative of Kapu's, 54–60; spirit
village and, 21. *See also* Symbolic
death (initiation)
Deep talk: Kapu's death narrative
and, 54–60; methodology for de-

159